MW00759797

THE MILLENNIUM HOUSE

PEGGY DEAMER
SEMINAR AND STUDIO
2000–2001
YALE SCHOOL OF ARCHITECTURE
EDITED BY NINA RAPPAPORT

THE MILLENNIUM HOUSE

THE MONACELLI PRESS

First published in the United States of America in 2004 by
The Monacelli Press, Inc.
902 Broadway, New York, New York 10010.

Copyright © 2004 The Monacelli Press, Inc.

All rights reserved under International and Pan-American Copyright Conventions.
No part of this book may be reproduced or utilized in any form or by any means, electronic
or mechanical, including photocopying, recording, or by any information storage and
retrieval system, without permission in writing from the publisher. Inquiries should be
sent to The Monacelli Press, Inc.

Library of Congress Cataloging-in-Publication Data
The millennium house : Peggy Deamer Seminar and Studio 2000–2001, Yale
School of Architecture / edited by Nina Rappaport.
p. cm.
ISBN 1-58093-123-5
1. Architecture, Domestic—United States—Case studies. 2. Architecture—United
States—20th century. 3. Architecture—United States—21st century—Designs and
plans. 4. Architectural design—Study and teaching—United States. I. Deamer, Peggy.
II. Rappaport, Nina. III. Yale University. School of Architecture.
NA7208.M54 2004
728'.37'0922—dc22   2003021600

Printed and bound in Italy
Design: David Frisco, New York
Editorial coordinator: Mark Gage

CONTENTS

FOREWORD
ROBERT A. M. STERN

Dean, Yale School of Architecture

The design of a single-family house for a patron of the arts may at first glance seem a less than urgent student project. But in truth, the problem opens up the architect or the architectural student to the possibilities of artistic exploration in relationship to landscape, spatial structure, and culture. This is especially true of a house undertaken to express a particular moment—a threshold between two centuries; indeed, the threshold between millennia.

At Yale, the thirty-year-old Building Project tradition involves first-year students in the design and construction of an affordable house in New Haven. The Millennium House seminar and advanced studio, led by Associate Dean Peggy Deamer, took on a different focus, interrogating the nature of dwelling in the postmodern world. With this seminar and studio, Professor Deamer brings to the fore the place of interaction between psychoanalysis and architecture. She also involves students in detail and fabrication at the level of craft, two preoccupations of her professional practice.

In the Millennium House project, students participated in a dynamic debate about ideas and also proposed a project for a real site and a real client, one with high ambitions for an artistic living environment. While technical and programmatic issues were addressed, the emphasis was on the meaning of architecture at a particular moment, our moment. This project is not a meditation on the past or the future but an attempt to define what is unique about the present. These circumstances notwithstanding, students were constantly reminded that they were designing for a specific client and a specific site.

Professor Deamer's seminar and studio were supported in part by Artur Walther, who also acted as the client, providing program and site. I would like to extend my appreciation to Mr. Walther and to The Monacelli Press for the second in the series of studio publications that document the work of the Yale School of Architecture.

THE MILLENNIUM HOUSE

PEGGY DEAMER

In his introductory essay to *The Un-Private House*, Terence Riley argues that houses today, as both a reflection of and a stimulation to domestic life, no longer divide public from private, work from home, community from family, outside from inside, culture from nature, commerce from leisure.[1] While this is hard to deny, the implications of these conditions for architecture are not clear. It is possible to agree with Riley but still insist (as Demetri Porphyrios did when arguing against the "new" architecture of Greg Lynn at a Yale studio review) that the fundamental aspects of daily life—we still get up, search for that cup of coffee, go to work, look forward to the solace of friends and family at the end of the day, enjoy good food, and appreciate a comfortable bed—have not changed, and so neither should architecture. Yet these and other considerations that remain fairly constant—the need for a house to establish a sympathetic relationship to the land, to mark the passage of time, to make seamless transitions between activities— need not imply traditional architecture. They can be accommodated and explored in unusual and unfamiliar ways. Ultimately, what is privileged as "essential" and how these "essentials" are deployed formally are both areas of discussion.

A man wanting to educate himself about the state of contemporary domestic architecture came to Yale hoping to examine some of these issues. He wanted to build a house for himself on a beautiful rural site, and he preferred to avoid the approach practiced by his friends—that is, choosing an architect who would make a new house appear as if it had stood for centuries, ignoring the fact that the sizes and accoutrements of such houses have never appeared in the areas where they are being built. Artur Walther believed—and I agreed—that technologies, lifestyles, and aesthetics have changed drastically since 1700. If he was to reject the standard approach, how would he educate himself and choose an architect?

The outcome of his questions was a seminar in the fall of 2000, in which Walther was a student, and a design studio in the spring of 2001, for which he acted as client. Every week guests visited the seminar to discuss particular themes: Bernard Cache on digital craft and topology; Steven Holl on physical craft and spatial phenomenology; Sulan Kolatan and William MacDonald on interior landscapes and single-surface geometry; Douglas Garofalo on blob architecture and topological geometries; Elizabeth Diller of Diller + Scofidio on "domesticity under surveillance"; Ada Tolla and Giuseppe Lignano of LOT/EK on "urban cyberpunk" and the house as found object; Craig Konyk on the changing house; Michael Bell on affordable houses, prefabrication, and industrial design; Jacques Herzog of Herzog & de Meuron on "the Miesian box and the changing skin"; Neil Denari on urban infrastructure and the house as urban machine; Winy Mass of MVRDV on the house as landscape; William McDonough on "the green box" and ecological architecture; and Craig Hodgetts and Ming Fung on "the house unfolded." Additional guests delivered lectures related to concepts of changing world views: Beatriz Colomina on the Eameses and their exhibitions of the 1940s, particularly *Glimpses of the USA*, and Barry Bergdoll on Mies van der Rohe's approach to landscape in his early houses. Walther's site and program then provided the content of the studio; as the client, he joined the critiques and reviews.

Three issues must be tackled in any consideration of domestic architecture. The themes of newness, uniqueness, and design innovation, though related, each have their own ideological baggage that must be considered by any architect. They all relate to the question of what it means to build at this moment in architectural time, and to the coincidence that this moment in architectural time is the beginning of a new millennium.

NEWNESS

Are identified changes in domestic life particularly "millennial"? As I planned the course, I considered the assumption that the new millennium was ushering in something revolutionary. As Riley identifies, and as is evident to many of those in the field, the computer and its relationship to advanced technologies and formal topological palettes are indeed new. Some of the architects visiting the seminar—Bernard Cache, Sulan Kolatan and William MacDonald, Douglas Garofalo—can thus be described as operating in the new millennium. But the year 2000 is no more than an arbitrary date in a continuum of change. Thus any emphasis on the millennium is ultimately more rhetorical than substantive, its purpose that of shaping, more than characterizing, the terms of the debate. Even as a rhetorical contrivance, however, the idea of the millennium served as a serious provocation about what is new or only appears to be new in today's architectural production.

One category within newness is the avant-garde. It is impossible to ignore the debate, initiated by Peter Bürger in his *Theory of the Avant-Garde* and contested subsequently by art critics such as Benjamin Buchloh and Hal Foster, about the potential of a contemporary avant-garde. Bürger claims that the avant-garde of the 1910s, 1920s, and 1930s—encompassing constructivism, dadaism, surrealism, futurism—was a unique event specific to a time when formal autonomy (art for art's sake, aestheticism) coincided precisely with an economic critique of the means of aesthetic production. Not only did Bürger suggest that this moment could never be repeated (and hence that a true definition of "avant-garde" would prevent the term from being applied to contemporary times), but he claimed that those posing as the avant-garde were, given the ultimate impossibility of overthrowing the very markets upon which art was dependent, doomed to failure.

In his "What's Neo about the Neo-Avant-Garde?" Foster, wanting to ensure a place for radical practices of an avant-garde kind, argues instead that the "failure" of the historical avant-garde leaves room for it to rise again in a more effective fashion—one in which the artwork's critique of the market is more sophisticated and savvy.[2] He points to Marcel Broodthaers, Daniel Buren, Michael Asher, and Hans Haacke as contemporary artists who produce works that satisfy Bürger's criterion of autonomous art able to disrupt the capitalist-driven mode of aesthetic exchange. The relevance for contemporary architecture is not whether Bürger or Buchloh/Foster is right; rather, these theorists, having defined the terms of the debate, make it impossible to glibly ascribe the adjective "avant-garde" to various architects' practices. For what is accepted on both sides of the debate is the idea that avant-garde practices are related not just to the production of form but to the disruption of economic systems of distribution.

It is easy to argue that architecture, unlike the fine arts, can never uphold this standard; art can avoid patronage and the museum, while architecture depends on clients with money and/or public endorsement. It is difficult to build an architecture critical of the society that is paying for it. Even if it is possible to hold out for a critical architecture, it is nevertheless necessary to acknowledge the complex web of social and economic forces that makes naive any claims of being an "advanced guard." Observers must be wary of architects and patrons who are awed by this designation. The issue of newness in this regard is not new, and it is not innocent.

Likewise, the haunting scepter of modernism must be considered in any investigation of newness. While architects believe, every time they sit down to design, that they are operating independently, freely, "newly," and while they believe that they are working from a post-postmodern perspective, the assumption that contemporary forms should match contemporary culture is essentially modernist. Moreover, the images that are foremost in architects' heads when asked to think of cutting-edge architecture are largely modern. The aesthetic battle between the box and the blob[3]—the former reinvestigating the Miesian and the tectonic, the latter exploring the digital and the representational—should not deflect an understanding that both owe allegiance to the modernist icon of the figural building negotiating its aesthetic, autonomous objecthood against a "natural" ground. Even more than this, the specific images of Mies that linger in so many of the currently privileged iconographic houses—Rem Koolhaas's Maison in Bordeaux, Preston Scott Cohen's Torus House, UN Studio's Mobius House, Kazuyo Sejima and Ryue Nishizawa's M House, Herzog & de Meuron's Kramlich Residence—suggest that there is nothing more modern than modernism. This recycling can be analyzed endlessly, but it must be pointed out that whether the reason is a continued interest in the aesthetic project of minimalism (Glenn Murcutt, Sejima and Nishizawa, Herzog & de Meuron) or surface (Greg Lynn, Bernard Cache, Peter Eisenman, MVRDV), in the technical problem of repeatability (Santiago Calatrava, Renzo Piano, Lynn), in the iconographic potential of modernism (Philip Johnson, Koolhaas, Cohen), or in the social program of democracy/transparency (Samuel Mockbee and his Rural Studio, Michael Bell, Koning Eizenberg Architecture), modernism, for better or for worse, still provides an operational model with unexplored territory. The role played by the icons of modernism in providing images of the "new" was an important concern in the seminar and the studio: it was essential that the students control them, rather than that the icons control the students.

UNIQUENESS

A second significant concern when considering the millennial is uniqueness. It is a natural assumption that, given a good budget, a spacious piece of land, and an adventuresome client, the architect will produce a special, one-of-a-kind house. But if a house is to relate to its era, it must be referentially broad, not merely singular; the more unique the house, the more limited its potential or symbolic (or actual) meaning. The prototype, that is, something that is repeatable regardless of site and client, takes the opposite position: a building gains significance through its implicit universality. The appeal of the prototype is the inverse of that of the one-off building: commissioning and/or designing an affordable and repeatable project links client and/or architect to mass, as opposed to elitist, culture. But just as extreme uniqueness limits a house's significance, extreme prototypicality can dissolve into the merely common. Something unusual needs to be present and the theme must be open to variation.

There are many versions of this conceptual tension—high design or low? limitless per-square-foot cost or affordability? special crafts or standardized modes of production?—and they all present ideological quandaries. However, it might be more fruitful to see the house as embracing both the unique and the universal, both the general and the specific. It is possible that something is unique not because it is singular but because it understands the potential for retooling rather than ignoring the means of production, not because it is unique historically but because it is repeatable technically.

Some architects who visited the seminar, like Bernard Cache, Michael Bell, and LOT/EK, actively explore productive repeatability and formal recycling. Others, like Jacques Herzog, Craig Hodgetts and Ming Fung, and Douglas Garofalo, are more interested in the arresting singularity of an exceptional house. A similar tension permeated the studio. On one hand, the studio "client" had the inclination and the money to build a "statement." It was hard for the students to resist indulging the specific site, budget, and client's dreams. On the other hand, the annual National Association of Home Builders convention in Atlanta exposed students to generic industrial products and conventional approaches to design. It was remarkable that the products, systems, and materials promoted at the convention, many of them technologically innovative, were used to simulate only traditional styles and outdated modes of construction. Sadly, "prototypical" was associated not with economy, efficiency, and repeatability but with the status quo and the lowest common denominator.

Certain problems inherent in the site also addressed the question of uniqueness. The one-hundred-acre plot in upstate New York was spectacular, unusual in its size and exposures. Supposedly, a site-specific house would be equally unusual. But on a more complex level, the site was also generic—typical, if not hyper-typical, of "nature." There arose a conceptual dichotomy, not necessarily productive, that allowed students to label the site as an abstract example of nature and also as unique. Even when the landscape is understood as constructed, manipulated, and culturally determined (in this case, it had previously been cleared and farmed but was sold and bought as a weekend property), there was no hindrance to seeing the site abstractly, as an example of nature as opposed to a place with specific views, smells, and ecologies. Indeed, Tom Phifer, an architect on the midterm review with a practice motivated by sustainability, was critical of this attitude as it was evidenced in the students' work.

But the problem of abstracting nature—of seeing it as more generic than unique—is one that seems to be inherent in contemporary architecture. In the examples presented in the seminar, this abstraction of nature was integral to the creation of an abstract house. Even in the work of William McDonough, who espouses green architecture, there is a sense that nature is a system, not a place. In addition, while many of the houses shown had a very specific relation to "landscape"—the landscape woven up and into the house; the house hovering above the landscape on piloti—they had a predetermined, a priori quality. Whether the house was a part of or apart from nature, the relative idealization was equal. This fact is not necessarily a problem; it may come automatically with recycling the modern, or with pursuing something prototypical. Nevertheless, it is worth noting that a hesitation to grasp the real specifics of a site is not currently, or perhaps has not ever been, unusual.

DESIGN INNOVATION

The third major concern in an examination of the millennial is the role of design and authorship. Design is the essential ingredient in any noteworthy project; indeed, the domestic program is considered the best opportunity for architectural/aesthetic experimentation, for yielding the most visible icons of architecture. But as Adolf Loos suggested, it is also the program most resistant to art and to the aesthetic urges of the architect. His vitriolic distaste for Josef Hoffmann's theory of *Gesamtkunstwerk*, the total work of art, in this case, the unified design of domestic space, is famous. Loos is known for observing that only two architectural programs warrant the application of "art": the monument and the urn. If the house is thought of as a place of personal retreat and unselfconscious activity, it becomes the last place for the application of external notions of design or art.

But a view of design/form as external to the needs of the client indicates a fundamental, and all too common, misconception of architecture as expensive and unnecessary. It fails to realize that design is already there, in every layout, in every furniture choice, in every construction detail; some design objects are just so familiar as to seem invisible. Within the act of design, formal manipulations have been conceptually separated from relational ones, stylization from organization. What Loos's critique does not acknowledge is that clients often do want their lives to be aestheticized, do want the privilege of formal virtuosity, do want the imposition of art. On the other hand, it is the rare patron who wants his or her life, patterns, and habits scrutinized, changed, or exposed. It is innovation in form rather than in domestic content that is interesting. This is one reason why houses architects build for themselves—where they offer for examination their own organizational patterns and domestic rituals—are a source of fascination.

During the seminar, students analyzed houses designed by the visiting architects to determine precisely where claims to innovation were being made, and whether they went beyond form to program and spatial hierarchy. In the studio, the existence of a real client made the question of design innovation more palpable. The students were caught between trying to please Artur Walther and unpacking the ideological assumptions behind his stated desires: a main building with two fireplaces (allowing cooking, eating, and gathering); three bedrooms with corresponding library/television areas, fireplaces, and dressing and bath areas; a greenhouse; and outbuildings including a three-car garage, pool and pool house, and two studio spaces. The opposition between pleasing a client and addressing larger cultural issues inherent in spatial/programmatic distribution is not uncommon in the dichotomy between practice and academia. However, working in the real world presents a slightly different version of this question: how much will an architect impose on clients given that the latter rarely want to address the larger organizational issues so important to the former?

THEORY, EDUCATION, AND PRACTICE

The issues of newness, uniqueness, and design innovation made a seminar and a studio that seemed so obvious and simple in agenda conceptually knotty and intellectually slippery. The reality of the situation—an actual client on a particular site—made the work richer, as did the students' own, sometimes conscious and sometimes unconscious, understanding of home life. While many of them believed that the beginning of the twenty-first century is witnessing huge technological changes that affect notions of place, intimacy, access, and transience, it was equally clear that domestic scenarios either had been mutating consistently away from traditional assumptions since the 1950s or in fact had never truly corresponded to those assumptions at all.

The studio, like the seminar, had weekly themes that required finished assignments. I wanted to thwart the usual process of moving haphazardly over the course of a semester from a vague initial concept to a concrete and specific one. I was also anxious to make research an essential part of the studio. The first assignment asked students to tackle the question of image. This topic paralleled a position discussed in the seminar: that modernist imagery is privileged in visualizing contemporaneity. The subsequent assignments were vehicles to rethink, refine, critique, and possibly reject those operative icons, which were then re-presented at the midterm and final. The weekly themes were image; site and object; skins and surfaces; standardization and modularity; plans, programs, and possessions; section and structure; light and the passage of time; networks and diagrams; site as infrastructure; and details and materials.

The last project of the semester was a book. This format reinforced the idea that the product of the semester's work was not a house—what the students designed was never going to be built—but a representation of a house, a simulation that would have its greatest didactic power organized according to the logic and narrative of a book.[4] The book also emphasized process over product. On one hand, the books documented the activities of the semester, a daily/weekly progress log. On the other, the books could function as manuals, instructing potential clients on how to put together a house—documents that matched and challenged the National Association of Home Builders handbooks for homeowners working without architects. As it turned out, these two aims would have corresponded only if the design of the students' houses was linear and cumulative, each theme refining those of the previous weeks; as it was, the students' designs often changed radically as the semester progressed, and the weekly log documented design vagaries, not linear development. Thus, many students, wanting to emphasize the final design, reworked their books at the end to present a somewhat false sense of logic. But the emphasis on the book and its record of the weekly work did serve the intended purpose: the final product is no more real, rich, or rarified than the investigation leading to it.

TIME

The millennium, the new, the avant-garde; the academic year 2000–2001; the modern, the postmodern, the post-postmodern; the fall, the winter, the spring, the summer; the morning, the afternoon, the night; the past, the present, the future: all of these modes of thinking about the passage of time were opened to the participants in the courses, whether as intellectual construct, institutional calendar, natural order, or historical chronology. But the events of September 11, 2001, have created a new sense of marking time, a deeply political one. While this might seem to diminish interest in something as innocent as architecture, there may be an even greater sense of the profession's role in constituting, changing, and symbolizing the political realm of culture. The scale of the buildings and the range of programs at the World Trade Center are seemingly unrelated to those of domestic architecture; yet the anxiety about rebuilding reinforces all of the concerns that arose in the seminar and studio: the role of form versus the roles of program and production; the relationship between culture and architecture; the dilemmas of uniqueness, newness, and modernity in a society anxious about stability, constancy, and security. The new millennium might prove that an architecture of the future should generate feelings not of cynicism but of hope—hope that the discipline adjusts to its newly found role of importance.

1
Terence Riley, *The Un-Private House* (New York: Museum of Modern Art, 1999).

2
Hal Foster, "What's Neo about the Neo-Avant-Garde?" *October 70* (fall 1994): 5–32. See also Benjamin Buchloh, "The Primary Colors for the Second Time: A Paradigm Repetition of the Neo-Avant-Garde," *October* 37 (summer 1986), 5.

3
This debate is outlined in Riley, *The Un-Private House*.

4
I borrowed this idea from Stan Allen, who in 1999 taught a studio for a prepackaged house at Columbia University Graduate School of Architecture, Planning and Preservation. He asked his students to design the manual for the house rather than the house itself.

THE MILLENNIUM HOUSE SEMINAR

BERNARD CACHE

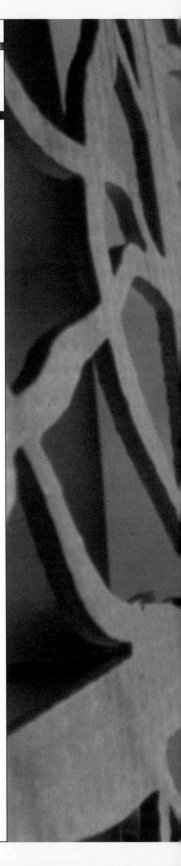

Our experience now enables us to think of a fully digital architecture like our museum project and the Philibert de l'Orme Pavilion we built for the Archilab conference in Orléans. The four elements of this pavilion are the result of experiments with screens, panels, and tabletops. In that process, we noticed that our approach had a clear affinity to Gottfried Semper's theories as articulated in *Der Stil* (1863), not only because we come to architecture through the technical arts, or because we invent new materials in order to create new designs, but because our interest in decorative wooden panels is consistent with Semper's *Prinzip der Bekleidung* (cladding principle). Even our investigations into the generation of software to map key elements of modern topology, like knots and interlacing, consist of a contemporary transposition of Semper's *Urmotive,* or primitive pattern.

Why focus on Semper, whose architecture seems to reveal nothing but the Renaissance historicism rejected by the moderns? Are we not in a very different period, one not of iron but of silicon? Why would we need to reconnect the end of our century of iron, concrete, and glass to the history of those of wood, stone, clay, and textiles? Do we not run the risk of a new technological determinism through which the information age, the so-called third wave, would create a second break with the past, definitively negating any historical experience, leaving us with no other alternative than a choice between the dinosaurs and the space shuttle? Or should we instead be reminded that information technologies themselves are deeply rooted in the past? The computer is not a UFO that landed one day in a California garage.

Semper claims that the number of abstract procedures is limited, which is why he is very parsimonious in counting them. Thus, metal is introduced as a material in itself, and right or wrong, Semper did not associate a specific procedure with it. Metal only provides another medium for the development of his abstract procedures.

Against all claims from Semper himself, the German architect maintained the very heart of the treatises of his Latin predecessors. What is so surprising in Vitruvius is his concept of transposition. Regardless of whether the motifs in stone, such as triglyphs, have their origin in wood, as Vitruvius claimed, or in fabric, as Semper would propose, the general principle is that the forms and proportions of the architectural orders are technically determined. Nevertheless, this determination does not come from the material but from procedures associated with another material, which have to be transposed. There is, then, a material determination in architecture, but it only appears through transposition, a process that manifests itself in the stone pediment ending the series of wooden trusses that support the roof of a Greek temple. The pediment transposes into stone the wooden structure of the trusses. The word "transposition" is the translation of what Semper had termed *Stoffwechsel* in German, "material transfor-

mation" in English, which brings us back to biology, since this was the word used by Semper's friend Jakob Moleschott to speak of the metabolism of plants and animals.

So rather than contradicting Vitruvius's theory, Semper raised it to a higher level. The origin of architecture is no longer unique, since it comes from the technical arts and, we might add, is no longer Greek. We could even say that there are no more origins but instead a composition of several lineages of transposition by which Semper's abstract procedures constitute themselves by switching from one material to the other. *Ut pictura architectura*. Vitruvius invents the transposition principle, but its application to tectonics in stone as a transposition from wood is just one step within Semper's general table. Architecture emerges in the move from one technology to another. Hence, textiles would today be the abstract procedure emerging from the transposition process, which leads us from primitive fabrics to contemporary modulation techniques while continuously emulating mosaic cladding, wooden panels, and embossed metal. Technical art is a contracting memory as opposed to an engram.

This text is adapted from *Digital Semper*, a lecture delivered by Bernard Cache at the Yale School of Architecture in fall 2000.

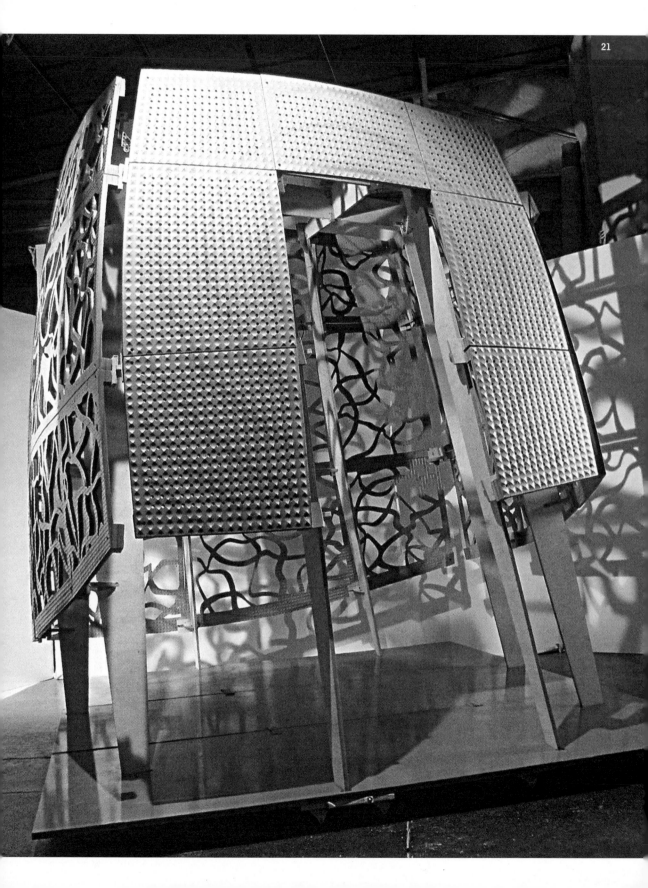

STEVEN HOLL

Simmons Hall

Massachusetts Institute of Technology, Cambridge, Massachusetts, 2002

The 350-bed residence is envisioned as part of the city form and part of the campus form. The Vassar Street side embraces the concept of "porosity." The building is a vertical slice of city, ten stories tall and 330 feet long, where urban amenities, such as a 125-seat theater and a night café, are provided. Dining is on street level, as in a streetfront restaurant with a special awning and outdoor tables. The eleven-foot-wide corridors connecting the rooms are like streets that happen upon urban experiences. As in Alvar Aalto's nearby Baker House, the hallway can be more like a public place, a lounge.

The "sponge" concept for the new residence hall transforms a porous building morphology via a series of programmatic and biotechnical functions. Five large-scale openings correspond roughly to the main entrances, the view corridors, and the main outdoor activity terraces, which are connected to facilities such as the gymnasium.

Slightly smaller openings create vertical porosity in the block with a ruled surface system freely connected to sponge prints, in plan and section. These dynamic openings (roughly corresponding to the residence units in the dorm) are the lungs of the building, bringing natural light down and moving air up in the building.

The PerfCon (perforated construction) structure is a unique design, allowing for maximum flexibility and interaction. Each of the dormitory's single rooms has nine two-by-two-foot operable windows. The deep wall naturally blocks summer sun but allows the low-angled winter sun to help heat the building. Different colors are applied to the head and jamb of the numerous windows, creating identity for each of the ten residence units within the overall building. The night light from the nine-window rooms is magical and exciting.

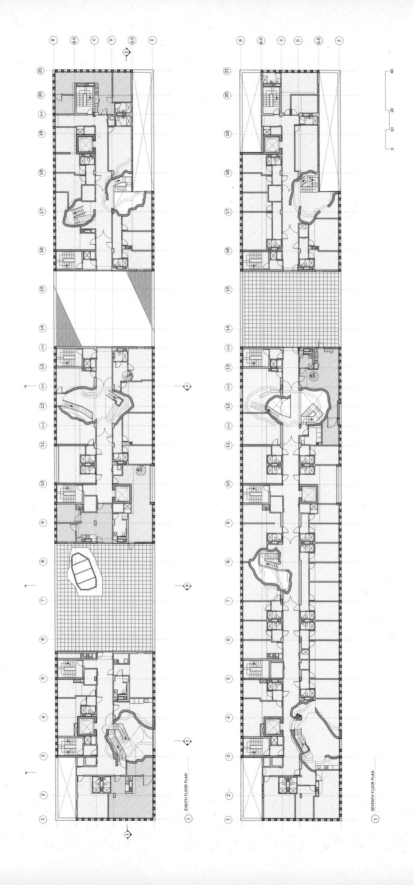

2 EIGHTH FLOOR PLAN

1 SEVENTH FLOOR PLAN

Y House
Catskill Mountains, New York, 1999

The Y House sits on an eleven-acre hilltop site with a panoramic view of the Catskill Mountains to the south. The design continues the form of the rising hill, splitting into a Y as it thrusts into balconies. The slow passing of time during the day will be unavoidably evident in the house as different areas are activated with the movement of the sun. The geometry allows sunlight and shadows to "chase still time."

The Y, like a forked stick, makes a primitive mark on the vast site while extending the view in several directions. The geometry of the Y enables a reversal in section of public-private and day-night zones. In the north half, the day zone is above and the night zone is below; the south half is flipped. The zones are joined in section by the central Y ramp.

The house occupies the hill and site through three primary relationships: "in the ground," "on the ground," and "over the ground." The portion over the ground is cantilevered above the portion in the ground, which opens to a stone court. The various slopes of the metal roof channel rainwater into a single water cistern to the north of the house. In the winter, passive solar collection occurs through the south glazing; deep porches shade the windows from summer sun. The steel frame and roof are iron-oxide red and the siding is red-stained cedar; interiors have white-painted walls and black ash floors.

KOLATAN/ MACDONALD

Architecture is competing on cultural and commercial fronts with the vast powers of themed environments, branded products, advertising, the Internet, and the music and film industries. We would like to propose a scenario whereby architecture adapts itself to new paradigms by adopting a cooperative mode at all scales to form selective, precise, and tactical chimerical systems with the fields listed above. We believe that the conditions for such mergers exist not only in contemporary structure-generating processes but also in the context of architectural tools and activities.

Computer-aided design and manufacturing software programs now constitute launching platforms for such diverse products as coffee machines, running shoes, cars, films, virtual and physical environments, and architecture. Thus, the tools for making, the processes of mental and material creation no longer differ fundamentally between product categories of the human-made. Contemporary architectural theory and practice have no choice but to address this generative convergence and its consequences.

Meta-Hom
Virginia, 2002
This ten-thousand-square-foot house for a couple with three grown children is embedded into a high point in two hundred acres of rolling hills in the Virginia countryside. We transformed the clients' desire for an open space with a series of columns into a continuous structure that combines floor, roof, and hollow cylindrical columns, creating a vertically porous house. This strategy provides a number of programs that relate to how hollow columns perform. The columns accommodate drainage (rainwater collection and recycling), circulation (car ramp into the garage, stair leading from roof level to lower terrace), and inhabitation (bath) as newly created opportunities.

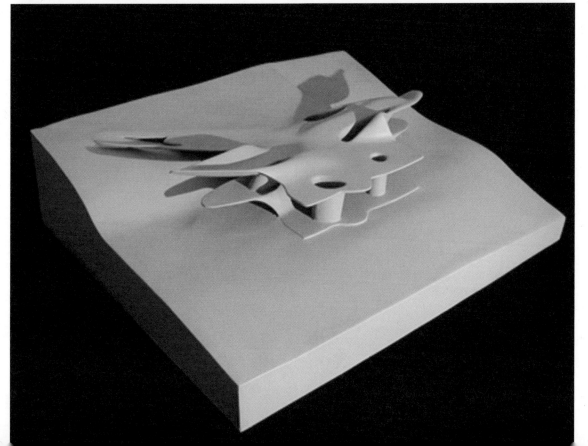

HaHouse
New York City, 2002

Designed for a Turkish couple with three grown children, this ten-thousand-square-foot house has an expansive view of New York City. Local regulations required us to keep the existing building envelope, but we turned it outside in using particularities of the site's topology, views, and wind patterns. The concavities of the core of the space act as membranes for the infiltration of light and air—typically exterior functions—into an otherwise deep section. The new and old perimeters of the building envelope index two different states of the house: one expands for the winter, the other contracts for the summer. During the summer, the concave spaces become fully exposed to the garden.

Raybould House and Garden
New York, 2002

Located on a four-acre site one hour north of New York, this 1,500-square-foot addition to an existing seventeenth-century saltbox house was planned as a weekend getaway and twenty-first-century "cousin" to the original. The house and garden converge to make the proposed addition. The construction methods combine boat-building techniques (defining the envelope with a series of Computer Numerical Controlled-cut ribs) and mowing strategies (trimming the foam in the sandwich of the monocoque shell with a machine akin to a lawn mower). Calculations for the house envelope indicate extreme energy efficiency: the interior can almost be heated with a single match and cooled with an ice cube.

DOUGLAS GAROFALO

While architectural design has always been central to my architectural practice, we believe that other pursuits—including building, producing exhibits and installations, teaching and collaborating with artists and academics on projects conventionally considered outside the realm of architecture—allow us to apply a more sophisticated grid of information to our architectural work. Much inspiration for current projects comes from other disciplines, particularly art and science. These are rather conventional links, repeated throughout history and for various programs/clients. Yet these general disciplines seem today to be intertwined in a myriad of ways, in particular through the use of digital technology, a sort of renewal of organic affinity through machines.

Our early work was not influenced by digital technology. In fact, our first commissions forced a reconsideration of a context for which most architects are taught to feel disdain—the American suburb. Yet we recognized that under the blanket of suburban homogeneity, contradictory forces of variation were at work. We designed a series of residential additions and renovations in Chicago's suburbs that questioned perceived ideas concerning the homogeneity of the context, and we found that the new face of this realm was increasingly ethnic, successful, and often not interested in any kind of building systems. These circumstances, coupled with stringent budgets and our own desire to resist the stylistic melting pot of suburbia, resulted in work that addressed and critiqued the idea of homogeneity. Our strategy was to propagate formal difference, mostly by taking existing elements and projecting them outward, instead of quietly aspiring to invisibility. Gradually, our interest in context became a sort of circumstantial emphasis that strove to study the nuances and subtle eccentricities within the supposedly regularizing tableaux of suburbia. The building materials and technologies of these projects are relatively simple and conventional: wood-frame construction, stock windows from a catalog, and the like. But the method of employing these materials and techniques is somewhat unconventional—these houses offer contrast and disjunction as a strategy. It is important to note, however, that in all cases we operated initially as detectives, searching for opportunities or clues: an oddly built structural system we could exaggerate, a zoning condition that might yield a useful contortion, an eccentric client request that could be emphasized or exposed.

In more recent work, we have moved away from the techniques and forms of juxtaposition and collage while trying to maintain certain critical sensibilities. This does not imply that issues of "difference" are less important. But heterogeneity itself is not a plausible quality to strive for, since it is always associated with a field, context, or discipline. We are now more concerned with the relations between disparate elements,

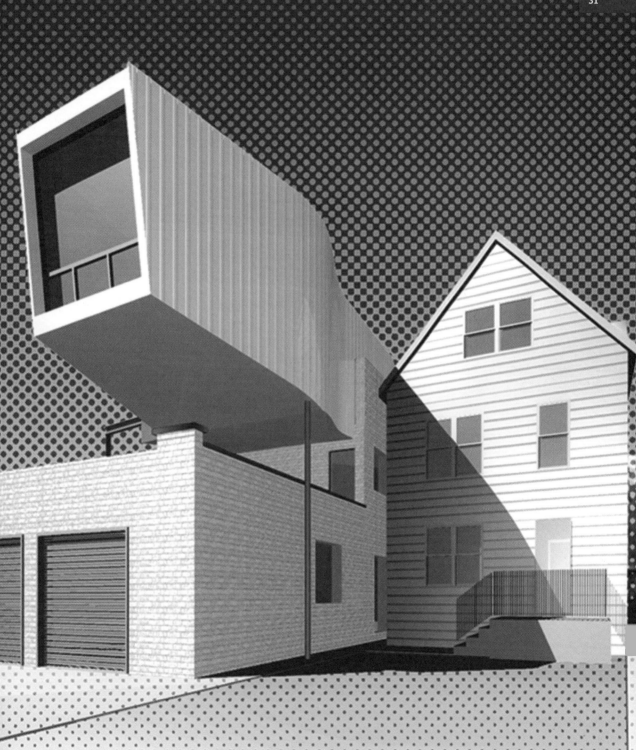

and it is perhaps more appropriate or useful to consider here the ecologist's definition of a "succession community." Succession refers to directional, cumulative change through time in the various species that occupy a given area. Through biotic heterogeneity (the state of being dissimilar or diverse), a community may be said to become more stable. The idea that stability may be measured in terms of diversity, complexity, and adaptability seems very foreign to the conventional idea of architecture as a static entity. What happens when hierarchy is no longer top down, no longer monumental or iconic?

As digital technologies continue to integrate architectural design and production, projects based on notions of complexity and adaptability grow more feasible, physically and economically. This shift has been accompanied by a growing interest in the effects of virtual tools on actual material. Such work involves thinking in terms of parameters, or any set of properties with values that determine characteristics or behavior. These properties are not static but vary across time (hence our particular interest in animation software). We are, like many others, interested in a kind of generative work, where the possibilities for architecture are considered in relation to movement, hybridity, event, repetition, and variation. To borrow a term from evolutionary biology, it might even be considered a certain "speciation" of architecture. This suggests neither buildings that move nor a new anthropomorphism for our discipline. Rather these issues engage processes of construction, opening up new techniques of craft.

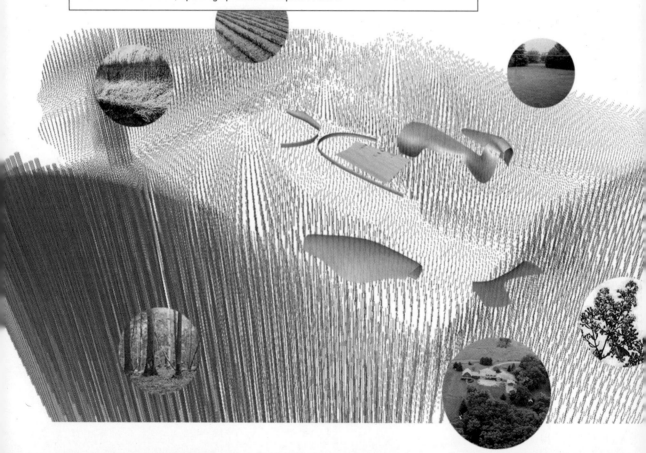

ELIZABETH DILLER

The Slow House

North Haven, Long Island, 1991 (unfinished)

The Slow House, conceived to produce a reflexive view, is situated in North Haven Point, the last undeveloped tract in the Hamptons, on Long Island. The area is populated by New York's migratory vacation culture, which, after World War II, cultivated the spread of European modernism and has continued to host many architectural experiments. "Perhaps more than any other type of architecture, the vacation beach house could be adapted to the radical new trends. Where the restraint might still have been considered appropriate in the year-round residence, a sense of adventure, experiment and abandon were more permissible in the design of the weekend house—especially if the house were sited along a beach," wrote Alastair Gordon in *Long Island Modern* (1987). It is possible that the seemingly contextless setting of sea and sky provided the architect and client with enough of a tabula rasa for the world to be remade. And since the vacation home was considered to be a "second" home, it somehow stood for a second chance— a chance to improve on the first home, to replay a life, to live out a fantasy.

The Slow House as a vacation home exploits the freedoms of the surrogate. Taking issue with the construction of visual pleasure for the leisure eye—both its production and its denial—the house regulates three optical devices of "escape" from and to culture: the car windshield, a reversible escape in the vehicular space between city and vacation home; the television screen, a solitary escape into the space of media, a social space that connects viewers with an electronic zone; the picture window, an escape into a proprietary scenic space, a space measured by market value. (The television screen, the architectonic of the electronic, and the automobile windshield were first related by Paul Virilio in "The Third Window," 1981.) Since the 1950s, the television and the picture window have been strongly allied in what Lynn Spiegel calls " the theatricalization and specularization of domestic space." Up through the 1960s, television and the automobile have been linked as paradigms of capitalist representation, according to Jonathan Crary in "The Eclipse of the Spectacle," "in the virtual annexation of all spaces and liquidation of any unified signs . . . The TV screen and the car windshield reconciled visual experience with the velocities and discontinuities of the market place." Today, the television and the car windshield, in conjunction with the picture window, can be thought of as escape valves into the white noise of vacation space-time. All three are used in the organizational logic of the Slow House: the television and the automobile oppose one another at extreme ends of the house, suggesting different infinities, while the picture window and the overlapping television flatten the receding space into pure surface.

The Slow House begins at the moment of departure from the city, the getaway. The automobile windshield frames the commute from city garage to country garage. When the car enters the two-acre site, it stops at the end of the road. The road terminates by deflecting up to support the roof plane, though the windshield view continues through a slot between road and roof. The glazed garage is at once storage space for the utilitarian machine and reliquary for the treasured artifact. The passage to the front door of the house resumes on foot. The house has no front facade; rather, the facade is a front door four feet wide and eighteen feet high. The clamlike outer panels open to a glass underlayer. Immediately beyond the entrance, a vertical knife edge slices the receding passage in half: one half leads to the right and ascends to the kitchen, dining, and living areas; the other remains level and heads to the left, to the bedrooms and bathrooms. The "slow" riser-to-tread ratio was based on that of the ceremonial stair leading up to the U.S. Courthouse in New York. Either choice in the forked passage leads to the picture window and continues through it to the water's edge.

The house deforms the model of classical perspective. The split passage is decisively anti-perspectival, with no direct visual axes, only constantly changing optical tangents splintering from the curve. As the axis of vision is bent, the formerly centered, unified subject in control of the world is teased off center, off balance. The house is a mechanism of arousal, eliciting an optical desire and feeding it, slowly. The only direct view is at the end of the hundred-foot-long wall, through the picture window, toward the horizon.

In the Slow House, the televisual view to the horizon is seen concurrently with, and compressed against, the view framed by the picture window. The television screen electronically reconstitutes the portion of the image that it blocks. The "view" is thus grafted together in two representational modes, though the horizon lines are out of register. Only one thing eludes the control of the passive viewer: the broken horizon can never be realigned. Thus the vacant leisure gaze is arrested at the window's surface and forced to contemplate the instrument of its contemplation.

The Slow House reconsiders issues of optical paranoia that emerged before the mid-1950s in the growing affinity between the television and the picture window. The designations "public" and "private" were called into question as television privatized the most public condition, the media, and the picture window publicized the most private, the interior.

Paranoia acquires a new face today—one more systematic of an "overexposed" culture: the fear that no one is watching. Yesterday's paranoia has become today's exhibitionism: we perform in front of the glass, we display our living room "sets" before the proscenium of the picture window, and so on. And we no longer regard the television as invasive. Rather we invite it to keep us company, to cook as we follow, to exercise so that we may join in, to help us shop, to set our eating and sleeping patterns. From early morning until late night, the synchronic paths of the picture window, the television, and the leisure body constantly intersect.

This text is adapted from *Flesh: Architectural Probes* by Elizabeth Diller and Ricardo Scofidio (New York: Princeton Architectural Press, 1994).

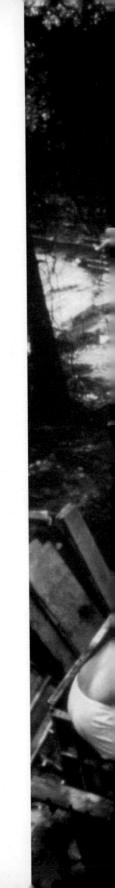

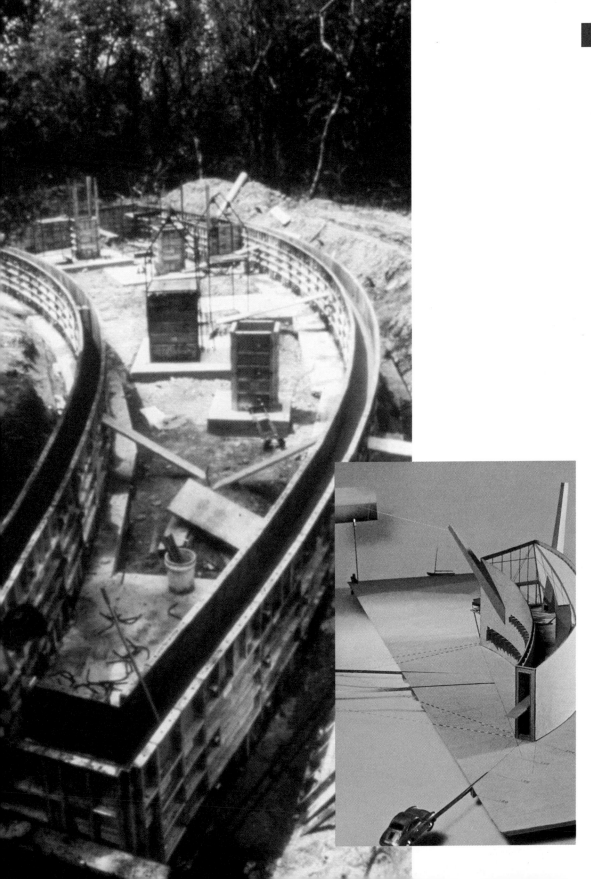

LOT/EK

MDU (Mobile Dwelling Unit), 2001

Cuts in the metal walls of a shipping container transform it into a Mobile Dwelling Unit. The cuts generate extruded subvolumes, each encapsulating a live, work, or storage function. When the container is traveling, these subvolumes are pushed in, interlocking with each other and leaving the outer skin of the container flush to allow worldwide standardized shipping. When the container is in use, all subvolumes are pushed out, leaving the interior of the container completely unobstructed. All functions are accessible along its sides.

The interior of the container and the subvolumes, including all fixtures and furnishings, are fabricated out of fiberglass. A central computer regulates airflow and temperature as well as lighting. It is connected with all communication networks and to monitors, speakers, and microphones distributed throughout the unit.

MDUs are conceived for individuals moving around the globe. The MDU, fitted with all live/work equipment and filled with the dweller's belongings, travels with its dweller to the next long-term destination. Once it reaches the destination, the MDU is loaded in vertical harbors. The harbor is a multilevel steel rack, eight feet wide (the width of one container) and varying in length according to the site. Its stretched linear development is generated by the repetition of MDUs and vertical distribution corridors. Elevators, stairs, and systems (power, data, water, sewage) run along these corridors.

Containers are inserted into slots in the vertical harbors by cranes that slide, parallel to the building and along the entire length, on their own tracks. Steel brackets support and secure MDUs in their assigned position, plugged in to all systems. The vertical harbor is in constant transformation as MDUs are loaded and unloaded. Like pixels in a digital image, temporary patterns are generated by the presence or absence of MDUs, reflecting the ever-changing composition of these colonies scattered around the globe.

Morton Loft
New York, 1999

A petroleum trailer tank cut in two provides the framework for the renovation of a loft space on the fourth floor of a former parking garage. The two segments encapsulate private areas, leaving the rest of the space undivided and unobstructed. One of the two sections is placed horizontally over the living room and contains two sleeping pods. Two large hatchback doors cut from each side of the tank bring sunlight and ventilation to those in bed. The second section is placed vertically from floor to ceiling. It contains two stacked bathrooms divided by a translucent horizontal plane. Metal grating catwalks give access at the mezzanine level to the upper bathroom, the sleeping pods, and closets on either side.

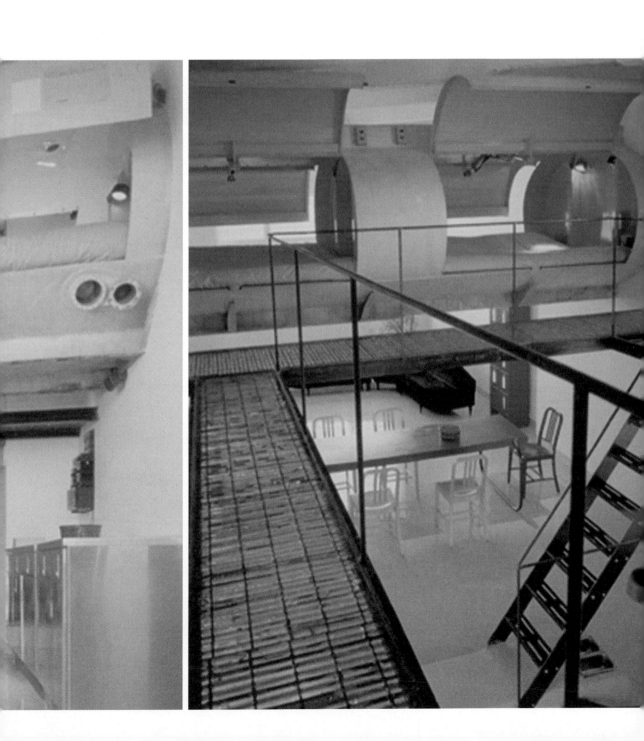

CRAIG KONYK

Hydra(one)
Project, 2000

Those in their sixties and seventies in the year 2000 came of age in the late 1950s and
the 1960s. These people embraced the youth culture of flower power and Volkswagen
Beetles, free love and Janis Joplin. They are not afraid to experiment with new lifestyles; they represent a cultural phenomenon. Approaching later years presents an
opportunity for this generation to once again invent and embrace an energetic, independent lifestyle of fitness, activity, and new accommodations. These individuals
will not go lightly into the night. They think of themselves as youthful, and indeed,
they are the most youthful mature generation ever. They will remain fiercely independent until the end, pioneers of the new spirit of a maturing America.

Accordingly, Hydra(one) speaks to this new situation of youthful maturity. A person
of this generation is more likely to drive a new Beetle than an Oldsmobile. The concept
house is designed to be a streamlined model built in the factory and assembled at
the site. Borrowing imagery and technical innovation from the aerospace industry and
Airstream mobile homes, the design evokes the spirit of mobility and the youthful
yearnings for travel. A thin skin of stainless steel is wrapped tight over a lightweight
steel frame, its singular surface a maintenance-free barrier to the elements.

The interior of the Hydra(one) model is sheathed in a layer of red neoprene rubber,
a material that is resistant to mold and mildew and wipes clean with a damp cloth.
The domestic functions of sleeping, showering, and food preparation and storage are
stowed along one edge of the volume; the facilities can be folded down or opened up as
necessary. In the default position, the interior is a seamless surface from ceiling to
floor, a pure volume of space, that can be used for any activity.

Atlantic City is the ideal locale to test-drive this new model of maturing. Situated
at the edge of the Atlantic Ocean, Atlantic City invented the boardwalk resort, a city of
casino riches and beauty pageants, a city of both Baltic and Pacific Avenues, a city
of exuberance. It is built on the mythology of leisure, of healthful ocean breezes. It is
here that the final quest for eternal youth may be sought.

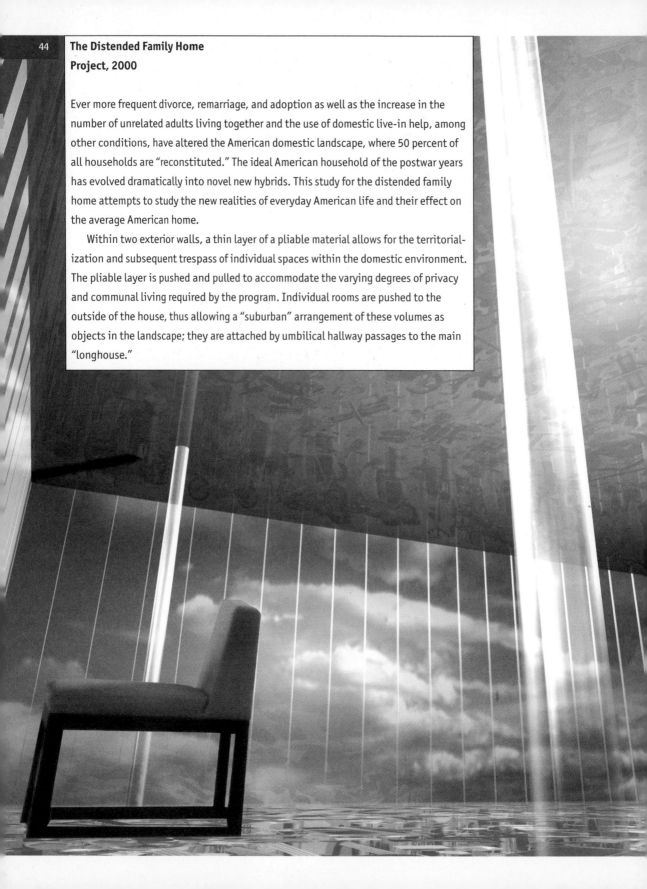

The Distended Family Home
Project, 2000

Ever more frequent divorce, remarriage, and adoption as well as the increase in the number of unrelated adults living together and the use of domestic live-in help, among other conditions, have altered the American domestic landscape, where 50 percent of all households are "reconstituted." The ideal American household of the postwar years has evolved dramatically into novel new hybrids. This study for the distended family home attempts to study the new realities of everyday American life and their effect on the average American home.

Within two exterior walls, a thin layer of a pliable material allows for the territorialization and subsequent trespass of individual spaces within the domestic environment. The pliable layer is pushed and pulled to accommodate the varying degrees of privacy and communal living required by the program. Individual rooms are pushed to the outside of the house, thus allowing a "suburban" arrangement of these volumes as objects in the landscape; they are attached by umbilical hallway passages to the main "longhouse."

BEATRIZ COLOMINA

We are surrounded today, everywhere, all the time, by arrays of multiple, simultaneous images—in the streets, airports, shopping centers, and gyms, but also on our computers and television sets. The idea of a single image commanding our attention has faded away. It seems as if we need to be distracted in order to concentrate, as if we—all of us living in this new kind of space, the space of information—could be diagnosed en masse with attention deficit disorder. The state of distraction in the metropolis, described so eloquently by Walter Benjamin early in the twentieth century, seems to have been replaced by a new form of distraction, which is to say, a new form of attention. Rather than wandering cinematically through the city, we now look in one direction and see many juxtaposed moving images, more than we can possibly synthesize or reduce to a single impression. We sit in front of our computers on our ergonomically perfected chairs, staring with a fixed gaze at many simultaneously "open" windows through which different kinds of information stream toward us. We hardly even notice it. It seems natural, as if we were simply breathing in the information.

How is it possible to write a history of this form of perception? It is not simply the military, or war technology, that has defined it. Designers, architects, and artists were involved from the beginning, playing a crucial role in the evolution of multiscreen and multimedia techniques of presentation of information. Take the 1959 American exhibition in Moscow. Site of the famous Kitchen Debate between Richard Nixon and Nikita Khrushchev, the exhibition was a Cold War operation in which Charles and Ray Eames's multiscreen technique was a powerful weapon.

In 1958, the United States and the Soviet Union agreed to exchange national exhibits on science, technology, and culture. Vice President Nixon, in Moscow in 1959 to open the exhibition, engaged in a heated debate with Khrushchev over the virtues of the American way of life. The exchange became known as the Kitchen Debate because it took place—in an event that appeared impromptu but was actually staged by the Americans—in the kitchen of a suburban house split in half to allow easy viewing. The Russians called the house "Splitnik," a pun on Sputnik, the satellite the Soviets had put into orbit two years earlier.

It was for this exhibition that the Eameses produced their film *Glimpses of the USA*, projecting it onto seven twenty-by-thirty-foot screens suspended within a vast (250 feet in diameter) golden geodesic dome designed by Buckminster Fuller. More than 2,200 still and moving images presented a "typical work day" in the life of the United States in nine minutes and a "typical weekend day" in three minutes.[1]

The film starts with images from outer space on all screens—stars across the sky, seven constellations, seven star clusters, nebulae, and so on—then moves through aerial views of the city at night, closer and closer, until city lights from the air fill the screens. The early morning comes with aerial views of landscapes from different parts of the country: deserts, mountains, hills, seas, farms, suburban developments, urban neighborhoods. When the camera eyes finally descend to the ground, we see close-ups of newspapers and milk bottles at doors. But there are still no people, only traces of their existence on earth.

Not by chance, the first signs of human life are centered on the house and domestic space. From the stars at night and the aerial views, the cameras zoom to the most intimate scenes: "people having breakfast at home, men leaving for work, kissing their wives, kissing the baby, being given lunchboxes, getting into cars, waving good-bye, children leaving for school, being given lunchboxes, saying good-bye to dog, piling into station wagons and cars, getting into school buses, baby crying."[2]

Like the Eameses' later and much better-known film *Powers of Ten* (1968)[3]—which, incidentally, reused images of the night sky from *Glimpses of the USA*[4]—the film moves from outer space to the close details of everyday life: "last sips of coffee" of men before leaving for work, "children washing hands before dinner," "housewives on the phone with clerks (supermarket food shelves in b.g.),"[5] and so on. In *Powers of Ten*, the movement is set in reverse, from the domestic space of a picnic spread with a man sleeping beside a woman in a Chicago park out to the atmosphere and then back down inside the body through the skin of the man's wrist to microscopic cells and to the atomic level. Even if *Powers of Ten*, initially produced for the Commission on College Physics, was a more scientific, more advanced film, in which space is measured in seconds, the logic of both films is the same. Intimate domesticity is suspended within an entirely new spatial system—a system that was produced by esoteric scientific-military research but that had entered the everyday public imagination with the launching of Sputnik in 1957. Fantasies that had long circulated in science fiction had become reality.

This text is adapted from "Domesticity in the Post-Sputnik Age," a lecture delivered by Beatriz Colomina at the Yale School of Architecture in fall 2000.

1

John Neuhart, Marilyn Neuhart, and Ray Eames, *Eames Design: The Work of the Office of Charles and Ray Eames* (New York: Harry N. Abrams, 1989), 238–41. See also Hélène Lipstadt, "Natural Overlap: Charles and Ray Eames and the Federal Government," in *The Work of Charles and Ray Eames: A Legacy of Invention,* ed. Donald Albrecht (New York: Abrams, 1997), 160–66.

2

From the working script of *Glimpses of the USA*, Eames Archives, Library of Congress, box 202.

3

Powers of Ten was based on a 1957 book by Kees Boeke, *Cosmic View: The Universe in Forty Jumps*. The film was produced for the Commission on College Physics. An updated and more developed version was produced in 1977. In the second version, the starting point is still a picnic scene, but it takes place in a park bordering Lake Michigan in Chicago. See Neuhart, Neuhart, and Eames, *Eames Design*, 336–37 and 440–41.

4

See handwritten notes on the manuscript of the first version of *Powers of Ten*, Eames Archives, Library of Congress, box 207. The film is still referred to as *Cosmic View*.

5

From the working script of *Glimpses of the USA*, Eames Archives, Library of Congress, box 202.

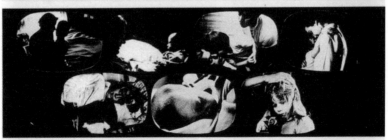

MICHAEL BELL

For the architect of public housing, professional practice has increasingly become concerned with a recuperative act of redistributing private and public space. In the *terrain vague* of the late modern city, form is a site of economic and political strife, and despite the domestic nature of the house—and the repose it hopes to offer—few types of architecture today are as driven by the commodity practices of the market economy. In the United States, the single-family house usually takes an overtly traditional form. While the financing and amortization processes of contemporary housing development are extraordinarily sophisticated, the construction and constituent components of its fabrication are shaped within low-level commodity and labor practices. The result is a housing market that is sophisticated as a speculative financial field but underwhelming as a site of architectural or material innovation.

Housing starts are one of the fundamental indicators of economic health in the United States, yet innovative modes of housing or even simple innovation in the design of housing are rare if not barely existent. In this context, alternative architectural practices in the United States are even more rare, but a prolific press and the recourse of an academic setting have allowed inventive firms to survive and to offer options outside the normal constraints of the market. Unlike the ambitious state-supported competition systems that award housing design contracts in many European countries, architectural commissions in the United States are almost uniformly an adjunct of market and speculative development practices. While this scenario has fostered the improved design and performance of commodities derived from large investments in research and development—such as computers, software, or automobiles—it has done little to improve the quality or innovation of housing. While housing financial practices are sophisticated, the material and labor practices of building are not. The results show themselves in every American metropolis and increasingly across the world as other nations emulate the American market economy in housing production. At this time, no nation has so fully relinquished the production of housing to market techniques as the United States, nor has any nation so fully protected the market as the source if not the curator of innovation.

The notions of closure and isolation that have characterized much of the public housing built in the United States since the 1930s are a legitimate and startling reason to seek alternatives to former federal initiatives. The trend to move public housing closer to market housing, however, brings an encounter with another set of complexities and indeed virtual forms of closure. The voucher system secures the market's rights to financial gains and applies this security to the production of housing—to the wealth and surplus accrued in housing production. Markets in this equation are expected to distribute not just form and material, or profits and land, but also domestic and

urban space within the predominant provinces and motivations of capital accumulation. For architecture this equation has often rendered the production of housing a site of political crisis, a negotiation between competing private interests, both of which describe their legitimacy in the political foundations of United States Federalist law. On the one hand, the federal government protects the market and what John Locke refers to as "men's different and unequal faculties of acquiring property." Some are assumed to gain wealth due to ability; others will not. The government also protects the rights to private property and wealth and the ability to enjoy its pleasures. Housing in the United States must sustain a conflicted coda between two modes of investment or a sequence of financial and private uses: the developer of housing seeks to extrapolate wealth from quick production; the house is used to produce profits. The second user, the eventual owner, seeks to secure and localize private wealth as well as maintain a psychological repose in the ownership of the property. The security of these pursuits—the rights of the market in regard to property—are, according to Locke, "the proper tasks of political society," and in this scenario they provide an essentially divided site. The role of the house or of housing changes: its initial role is brief—between production and sale it is a speculative venture intended to quickly harness wealth. Its secondary use is of longer duration. Here the house is intended to provide the closure and security of dwelling.

This text is adapted from *16 Houses: Designing the Public's Private House*, by Michael Bell (New York: The Monacelli Press, 2003).

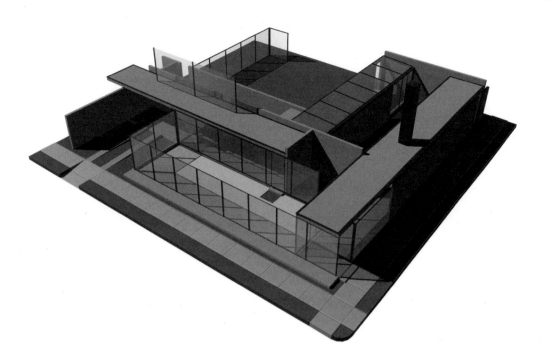

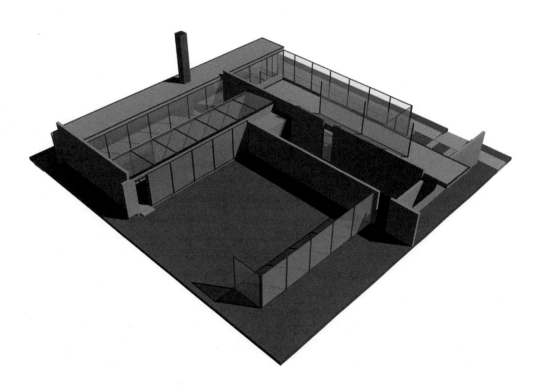

JACQUES HERZOG

Kramlich Residence and Media Collection
Napa Valley, California, 2000–

We met Pam and Dick Kramlich through Christian and Cherise Moueix, our clients for the Dominus Winery in Yountville. Cherise told us that, unlike many art collectors in Napa Valley, the Kramlichs collect media art, such as video, films, CDs, slides, and the like. Over dinner in a noisy restaurant, we spoke almost exclusively about the videos Pam and Dick had acquired. We were impressed that established and affluent people would choose to focus on media art instead of succumbing to the temptation to collect "real," that is, traditional, tangible art that can be put on display. This uncompromising commitment surprised and fascinated us and later inspired a radical architectural approach to the task at hand: a residence that would also be an exhibition space for media art or, conversely, an inhabitable media installation tailored to meet the daily requirements of Pam and Dick Kramlich. Was it a home as a media installation or a media installation as a home?

Our initial idea was to unite life and art, rather than separate them as usually happens in media art. The alienation caused by darkened and wired rooms full of technical apparatus all too often leads to a break between viewer and artwork, which would be aggravated and even more alienating in a home. We tried to devise a spatial concept that would structure but not completely separate the various areas and needs of daily life: one single space with places of different characters that can, in part, be set apart as intimate niches or more open areas. Our architectural treatment of the space allows exterior, interior, and artists' projected images to flow into each other.

From the beginning, we worked with the idea of curved, glazed walls because the curvature of the walls both enhances continuity and structures space while the transparency of the glass both reveals the structure and allows it to be experienced as part of a greater whole. We love this dual function of glass. On one hand, it verges on "nothing," on total transparency, on the absence of materiality. On the other, its materiality is evidenced in the boundaries of the room, which become visible where the curved walls intersect. The reflecting quality and curvature of glass underscore both the visibility and the invisibility of the material.

In the first sketches, the curved system of walls was enclosed in a rectangular system. We rejected this layout because we wanted to relate and blend inside and outside in a way that cannot be achieved with the classic binary form of juxtaposition. In subsequent sketches, all the longitudinal walls follow an undulating line so that inside and outside walls intersect, forming chambers for various uses. We finally came up with a concept for one large, undivided space with no hallways or adjoining rooms. The result

EXISTING GRADE

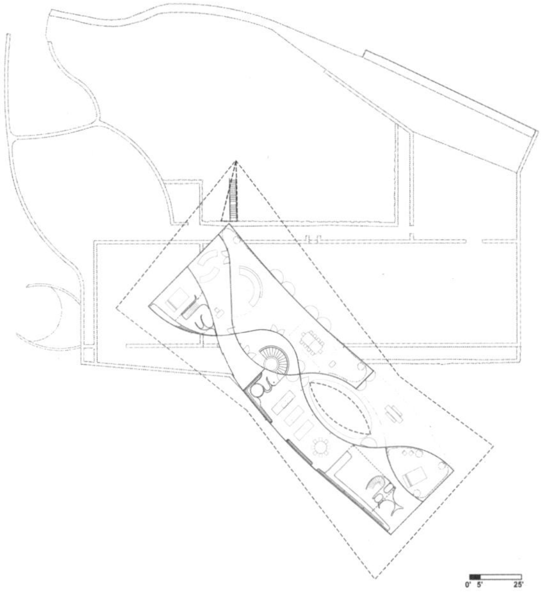

+18'-0"
+15'-0"

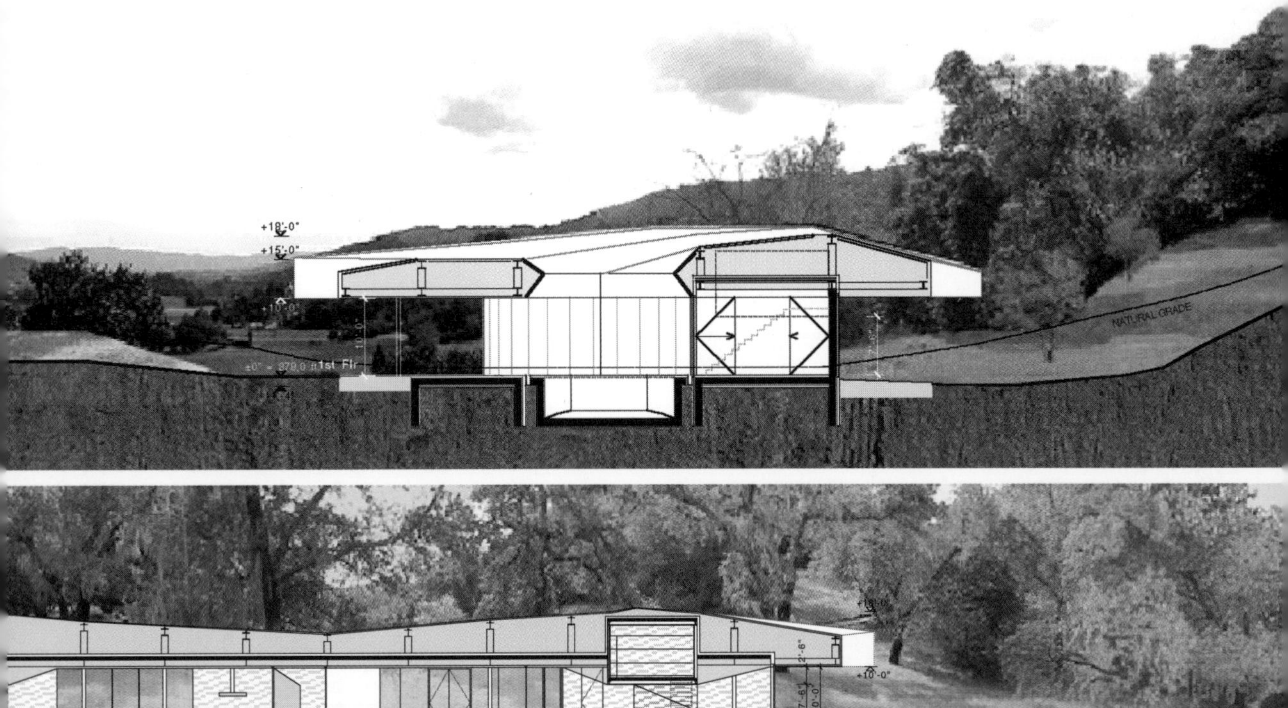

±0" = 378.0 1st Flr

NATURAL GRADE

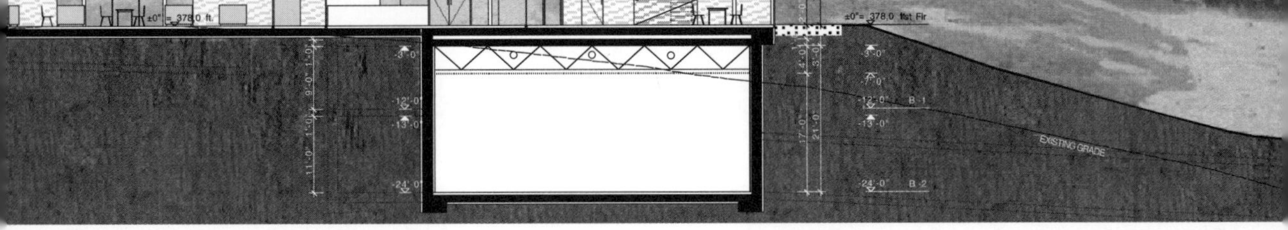

±0" = 378.0 ft.

+10'-0"

±0" = 378.0 1st Flr

EXISTING GRADE

is a spatial continuum, open, flowing, and unified, that also incorporates a merging of space that meets the requirements of privacy. Since our spatial concept was developed from the inside out, we did not at first focus on the exterior appearance of the house. As it turned out, the space generated by the curvature led to a fish-shaped whole. However, we did not want a figurative analogy of this kind and realized, in fact, that we did not want a building at all, or rather not a distinctive building that would immediately be identified with a specific shape. So we had to find a way to play down its figurative and physical presence. The only viable solution was to project the roof as far as possible. The first models provided compelling confirmation of this insight. Under this roof, the seemingly organic shape suddenly dissolved back into single curved walls, intersecting with other curved walls as they proceed through the house, thus generating chambers of various sizes and shapes.

House

Leymen, 2000

The exterior shape of the house recalls a prototypical house. A sloping roof, a tall chimney, and large windows resemble a child's drawing. The tar-board roof and the unfinished concrete facades flow almost seamlessly into one another. The simple, monolithic building is exposed to wind and weather; rainwater runs down the structure as it would run down a boulder. The unfinished concrete walls emphasize the weight and materiality of the building, but the house is raised off the ground, as if on stilts, which lightens its appearance. The projecting decks at the sides of the house reinforce this image of lightness and of suspension over the landscape. Fruit trees and meadows underline the agricultural character of the garden, which is barely distinguishable from the surrounding landscape. The interior of the house is characterized by contrasting spatial qualities and materials, such as concrete, adobe, and colors like silver and pink.

NEIL DENARI

Consider two glass houses: the Farnsworth House and Apple's iMac computer. The famous house built by Mies van der Rohe in 1951 was designed from the inside out. It was an attempt to radically rethink the spatial program of the domestic environment: no walls, no opacity, only glass and furniture; no scopic limits, only ever-changing seasonal views of the Plano, Illinois, countryside; no public, no private, everything the same; new functional demands, no formal ones. The famous computer from Apple was designed from the outside in: no change in computer performance, but a big change in market performance; no beige, only see-through colors; no expandability; no boxes, only perfectly contoured ovoids; new formal demands, no functional ones.

The two houses offer compelling evidence that the split between traditional modern architecture programs (room/space functions, furniture locations, storage, etc.) and market-based programs (styles, forms, colors, effects, etc.) still offers enough fuel for the form-function debate. The extent to which form, as reflected in an exotic envelope, for instance, can be described as functional depends on the understanding of use. Clearly, at the dawn of a new millennium, with the turbulence of politics and money defining the contemporary field of play, the house needs to respond to as many aspects of life as possible.

Where strict concepts of function limit precision to ergonomic relationships, basic building systems and components, and more resolutely, an indifference to formal expression outside the discourse of problem solving, other possibilities of function can generate precise ideas of another kind. If the vagaries of market economies and the recurring challenges of what Norman Foster called LL/LF/LE (long life, loose fit, low energy) in the 1960s are crossed with a general exploitation of the experimental nature of architectural form and space, then the intensity of solutions for dwelling may reach what has always been the most powerful description of the house: a slice of the city, complete with centers and peripheries, differences, and repetitions.

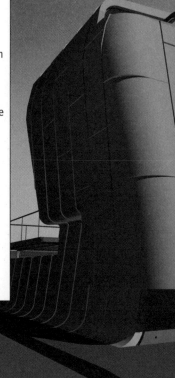

Indeed, the performance aspects of the house must rise to new and unprecedented levels: the house must capture the unfettered feel of innovation. Mies envisioned new "psychical" relationships in the house in the same way that the iMac changed the perception of the relationship between function and market-based packaging. If these two glass houses were to be hybridized, it might be the beginning of something entirely new.

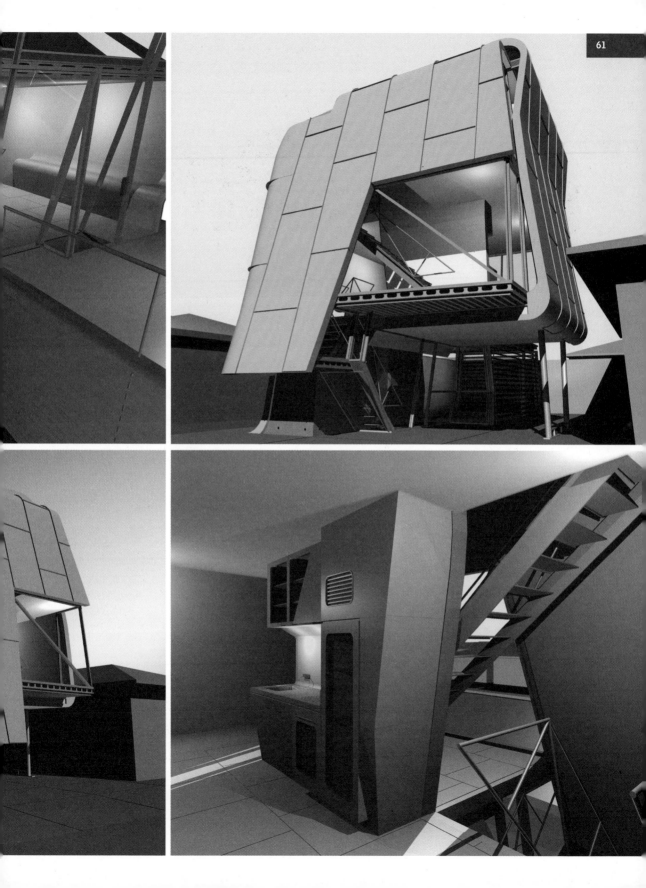

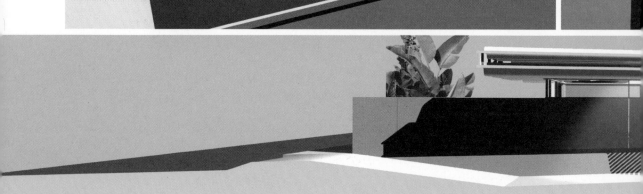

BARRY BERGDOLL

Since the mid-1980s, a new chapter in the critical reception of Mies van der Rohe, much of which has centered for the first time on the experiential aspects of the Barcelona Pavilion, has opened up new questions about Mies's practice in relation to nature, consciousness, and shifting attitudes toward technology—a series of questions that have cast his practice not only as critical but as critically engaged with issues that still confront architecture today. Perhaps Mies did not need to go around back to the corner of Schinkel's museum, which Mies scholars in the 1950s helped render famous with the shared tectonic interest that Schinkel called "giving to visibility" and Mies "the appearance." Perhaps Mies indeed learned as much from the jutting stair behind a colonnade that served as a frame for positioning Berliners in a panoramic dominance of their own city—it pictorialized Berlin—as he did about the representation of an essential architecture.

Mies at the Riehl House does exactly what Schinkel did in the Schloss Gleinicke: the space excavated under the portico is an extension of the dining spaces within, even as the facade is an extension of the great wall that articulates the spaces of the exterior and divides the two views of the house so that they are never experienced simultaneously. In the same way that the portico of Schinkel's Charlottenhof was created for al fresco dining, so the Riehl House's portico is not only a place for individual contemplation of the landscape but a continuation of the interior spaces of entertaining (fully equipped with a small dining table, an upright piano, and the first of Mies's outdoor curtains for regulating light levels and privacy). The great wall that extends the space making of the house across the landscape makes a curious step up at precisely this point to eliminate the foreground from the view for the seated viewer, pictorializing and distancing the contemplation of nature. Indeed, as is evident in the photograph of Mies himself at the house, a seated viewer would perceive only sky and treetops, a dramatic reinforcement of the precipitous site of the house.

Even as Mies declared in a speech celebrating the anniversary of the German Werkbund in 1932, "We want to investigate the potential residing in the German space and its landscapes," his American champions systematically weeded out from his plans the wiggly natural lines of both exterior vines and household plants. And the trees framing the rear facades at both Barcelona and Brno were eradicated, leaving plans that spoke for a vision of autonomous, universal space, internalized and reproducible anywhere.

These erasures not only fundamentally altered the nature of Mies's spaces but blurred traces of a historical line of development. In place of a meandering path that ultimately led back to Mies's interests in the vibrant reform movements that animated discussions of house and garden about 1905–10, the years he was establishing himself

in architectural practice, was drawn a rapid, unhesitating trajectory of avant-garde invention and artistic independence.

Key to this new philosophy was the idea of open-air rooms, which were meant to extend both the spaces and the functions of the interiors into complementary exterior spaces, not only in living and kitchen gardens but also in gendered gardens adjacent to the men's study or smoking room and the lady's parlor and in special gardens for children. Adopted by proponents of sanitary reform and of free-body-culture, or nudism, these open-air rooms were to sponsor a whole new mode of physical and spiritual life.

Mies went beyond fulfilling the period's concern with benefits to body by developing the ideal of the house as a frame for both spiritual well-being and the practice of philosophy. The exploration of a dialect between interior and exterior is developed at several scales. The house/garden podium takes up only the upper third of the site.

Mies created a house that stages a discovery and engagement with the larger environment, one that seems already to place his exploration of architecture in dialogue with Riehl's neo-Kantian definition of modern philosophy: "Instead of dealing with nature, which is the object of experimental investigation, philosophy deals with the condition of the knowledge of nature." Yet there is no more of a direct connection to political events in Mies's work than there was to the distant contemplation of nature he proposed as a palliative to the larger modern condition. In the most developed of Mies's designs in which interior and exterior spaces are bound into an inextricable dialogue by a bounding perimeter wall, that perimeter serves the same purpose that garden walls of either mineral or botanical form had always fulfilled in the architect's designs. They were devices for controlling the vista and for making integral to architecture a contemplation of the horizon, of what lies just outside daily existence but is readily accessible to heightened consciousness.

This text is adapted from "Siting Mies: Nature and Consciousness in the Modern House," a lecture delivered by Barry Bergdoll at the Yale School of Architecture in fall 2000.

WINY MAAS

100 WOZOCOS (100 Houses for the Elderly)
Amsterdam-Osdorp, Netherlands, 1997

The western garden cities of Amsterdam, built in the 1950s and 1960s, are currently confronted with big increases in density that threaten their open green spaces, the most important characteristic of these parts of the city. A block of one hundred apartments for people over the age of fifty-five was proposed to mark the end of a strip of housing for the elderly. This block was to supplement existing housing typologies for the elderly. The apartment could offer its inhabitants more independence; after the "gray wave," such dwellings could accommodate younger residents as well.

To provide adequate sunlight for the surrounding buildings—in accordance with Van Eesteren's AUP regulations—only eighty-seven of the hundred units could be realized within the block. If the remaining thirteen were placed elsewhere on the site, the open space would be further reduced. A deeper block with narrower units did not seem a viable alternative, because the north-south orientation of the block meant that the module had to be 7.2 meters. So we cantilevered the last thirteen units from the north facade; they are literally suspended in the air. The east-west orientation of the hanging apartments provides the north-south dwellings in the block with a view over the adjacent polder.

An economical layout for the main block saved 7 to 8 percent of the cost, enough to compensate for the hanging units, which are 50 percent more expensive. The spartan gallery flat becomes acceptable. Each gallery has a different perspective. The apartments acquire their own character with different window positions, balcony sizes, and balcony materials.

Party walls were constructed eight centimeters thicker than structurally necessary for sound insulation, and we used this extra thickness to connect the cantilever trusses so that the weight of the load-bearing walls did not have to increase. Sound and fire regulations made it necessary to clad the trusses. The ground plane is kept as open and green as possible.

Two Houses in Borneo-Sporenburg
Amsterdam, Netherlands, 2000

Plot 12

In Borneo-Sporenburg, a compact new housing district in Amsterdam, we designed two dwellings with the greatest possible spaciousness and versatility within a limited envelope. Plot 12 was designed in collaboration with Arno van der Mark. The house was built on a narrow plot, five by sixteen meters; the design used only half the plot's width, resulting in a private alleyway and the narrowest house imaginable. The master plan for the district, which divided the land into strips, is here carried to an extreme.

The length and height of the house along the alley have glass facades, while the front is entirely closed; thus, the house turns to face the alley. The composition of spaces is extremely varied. Interior and exterior are one: an extremely narrow house becomes an extremely wide house. The alley accommodates three elements: a block for storage with a roof that slopes up from the street and provides a place to park; a closed block for a guest room and bathroom; and a closed block that provides extra width to the two studios on the first and second floors. The two closed volumes are hung on the glass facade to enclose the exterior space and enliven the alleyway. Outdoor lighting allows the interior to have many levels of illumination, so the use of electric lights is avoided inside.

Plot 18

Plot 18, a garden plot in Borneo-Sporenburg, is 4.2 meters wide and 16 meters deep with a 4-meter-deep garden on the water. In principle, the 9.5-meter-high envelope allows for only three floors—one high floor at street level and two lower floors above. Despite this, the plan has four floors, and the ceiling height over much of the building is higher than normal. "Sliding out" one of the four floors facing the water at the rear creates a spacious long cross section with two closed elements: a garage/storage space on the street and a protruding bathroom/bedroom block on the second floor. The irregular space remaining contains the kitchen and dining area, sitting room, and study, which are all spatially connected to one another.

The rooms differ in height and degree of privacy. Each is connected with the exterior in its own individual way: a two-story veranda facing the water, a balcony with French windows outside the living room, a glass bay window in the bedroom, and a roof garden in the "attic."

THE MILLENNIUM HOUSE STUDIO

IMAGE

The first topic for the studio was the image of "house" in terms of representation, visualization, and seductiveness. The ability—indeed, the insistence—of the image to both precede and supercede the act of construction made it an important element in any inquiry into the nature of the house and domesticity at the turn of the millennium. It was essential to remember that the traditional image of "house" is very powerful and almost unavoidably, subconsciously, influential. Moreover, since the final outcome of the studio was to be images, not a building, it was important to establish this theme early in the process.

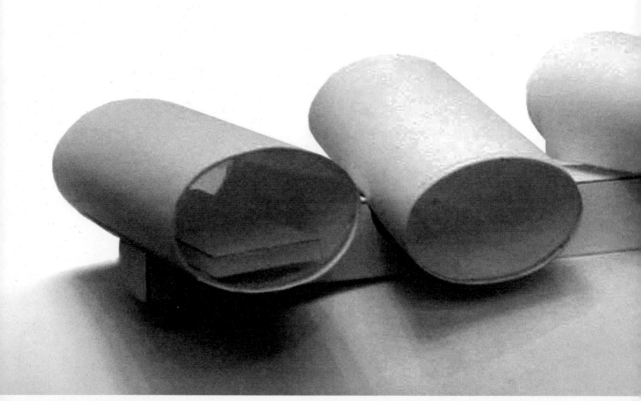

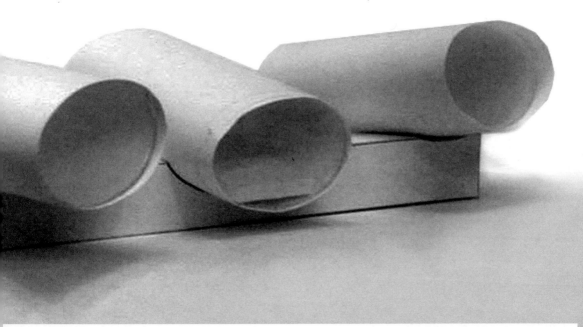

The image of the millennial house is represented by the division of the program into distinct categories of differentiated parts with one systematic organization. These categories are housed in equally sized "rigatoni" connected along a transverse bar. The tubes have the ability to relate differently to the site: some lodge themselves into the ground, some simply touch the ground, some hover above the ground. Furthermore, the tubes tilt in various directions along their vertical axes and twist along their common transverse axis, framing different views of the landscape. The emphasis of these objects is on perception and consequently on the occupant. It is only in "filling" the "rigatoni"—human occupation—that they become useful.

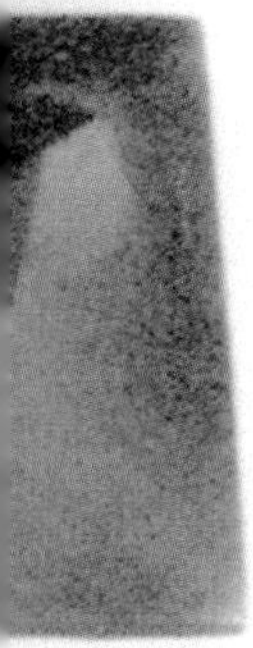
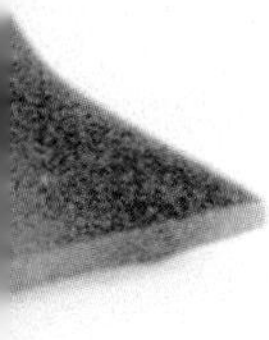
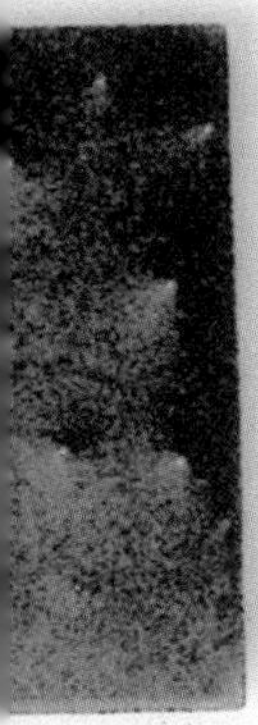
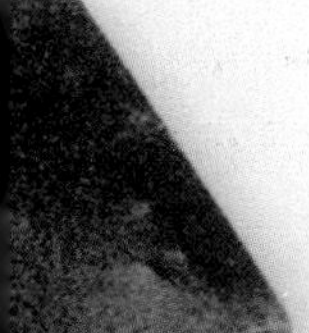
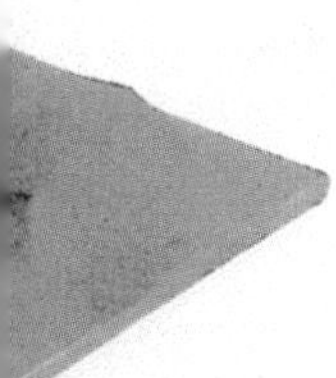
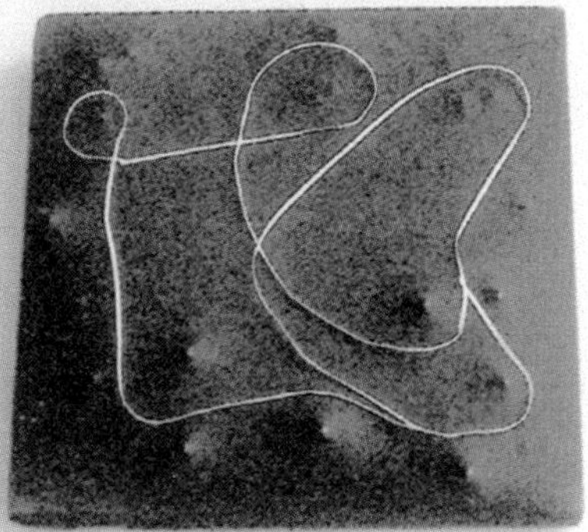
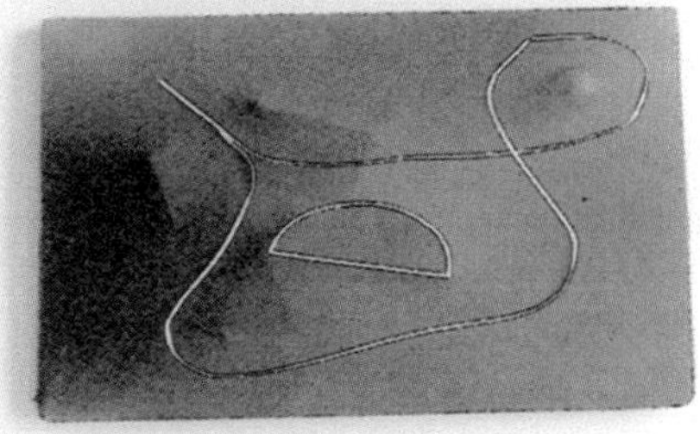
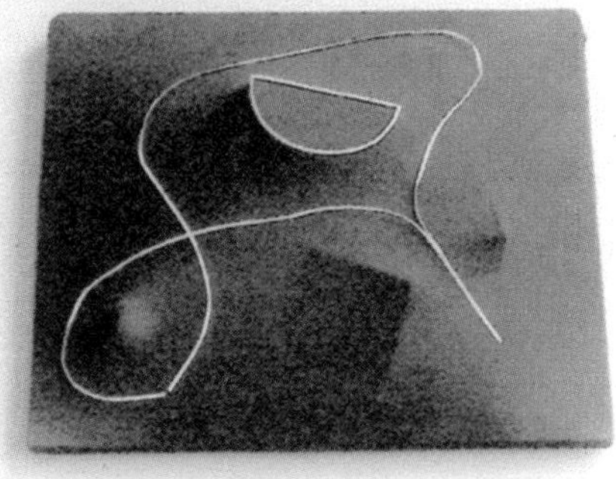
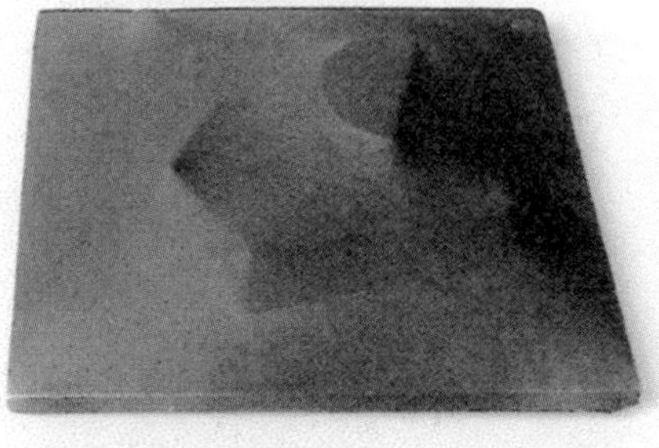
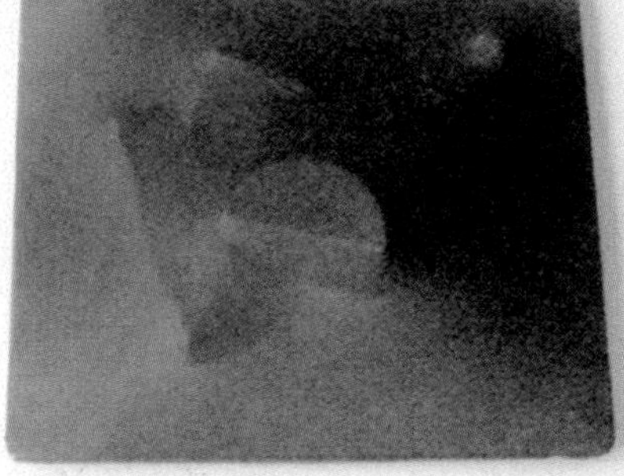
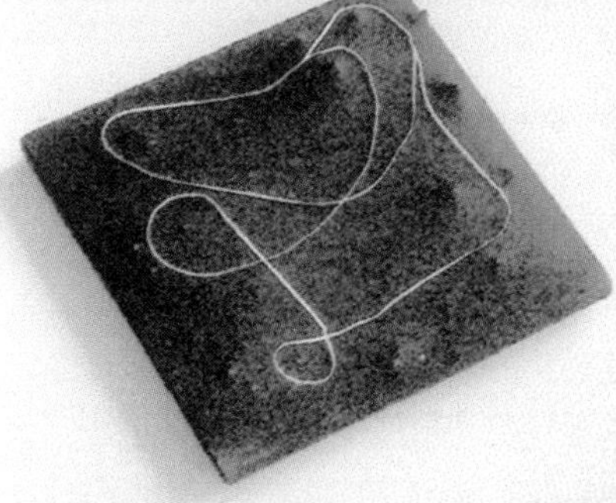
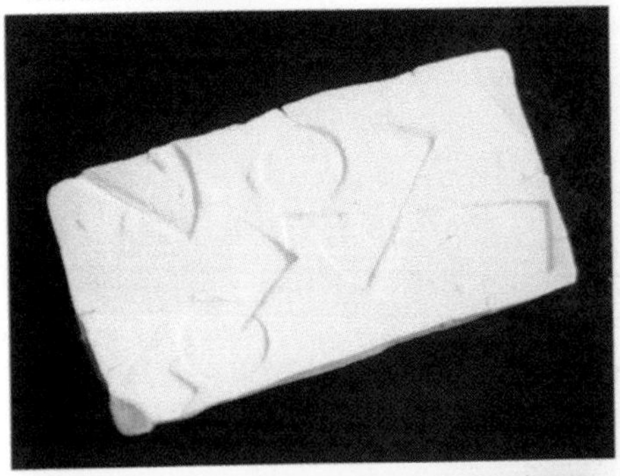
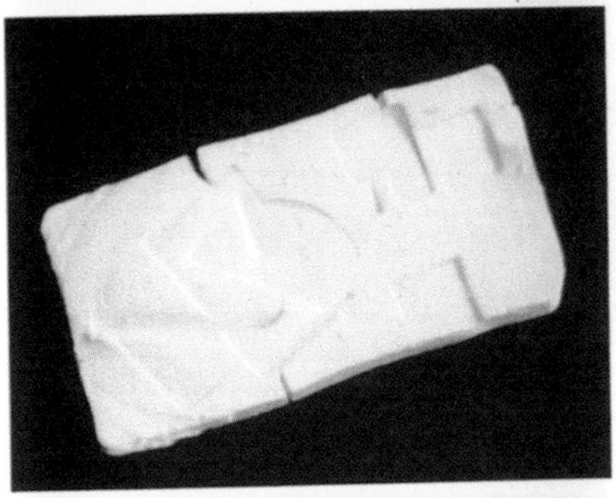
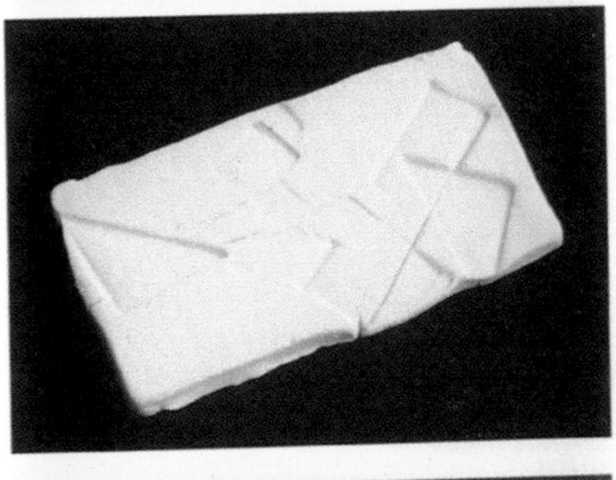
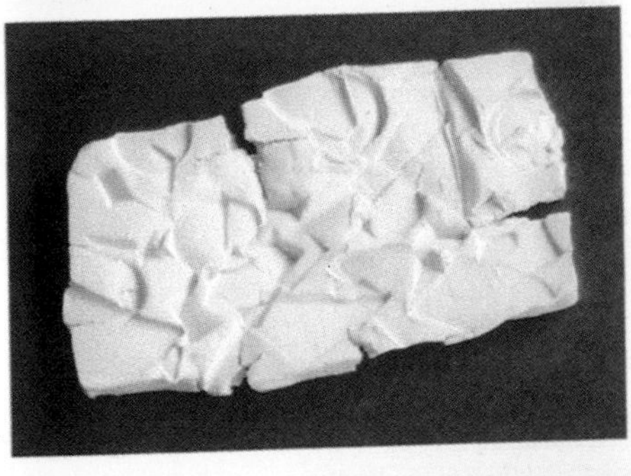

The house is both a continuation and a denial of nature. The connection is indicated by the design, which proposes a seamless procession from the land up, onto, and around the house. The discontinuity is indicated by the materials, only simulacra of what is found in nature.

The rapid development of technology has reshaped the way people live. Telecommunications and networking provide the ability to interact with people and places at every moment. The concepts of time and space have changed; working and living have been reintegrated. The house, formerly just a long-term residence, has become a living station to accommodate all needs. It can be anywhere and everywhere—its position is determined less by its lateral position on the earth than by its vertical position between a satellite and the earth's surface. The house must register its "landing" on the earth.

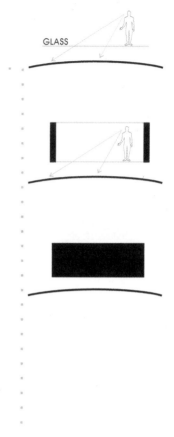

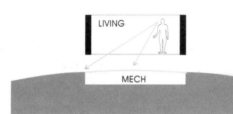

The millennium house is conceived as an arrangement of dematerialized fragments of the site—sites instead of rocks. This arrangement affirms the stealth materiality of the earth. The secret of the millennium house is its uncertain physical existence.

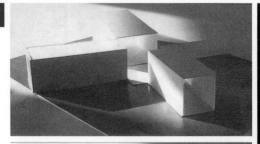

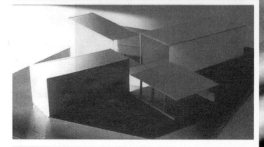

The house of the present is not different from the house of the past. The main question remains the relationship between house and environment: the degree of exposure and enclosure; the passage of light throughout the day; the closing and opening of views.

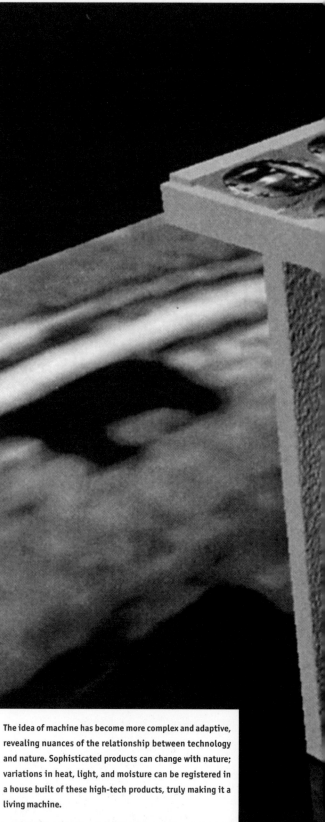

The idea of machine has become more complex and adaptive, revealing nuances of the relationship between technology and nature. Sophisticated products can change with nature; variations in heat, light, and moisture can be registered in a house built of these high-tech products, truly making it a living machine.

The house is experienced not as an isolated object but as part of a sequence that begins with the approach. This house is part of the procession from and through "nature" and is therefore ultimately bound to the land it occupies since it orchestrates arrival to and passage across the land.

SITE AND OBJECT

After studying the program and location for the Millennium House, two potential attitudes toward the site came to the fore: first, to see the house as an object located in, but separate from, the landscape; second, to intertwine the house with the landscape. The first viewpoint is perhaps more Miesian, the second more Deleuzian. Barry Bergdoll's lecture in the fall semester seminar emphasized that Mies's houses were always intimately connected to the landscape, even those that are seemingly divorced from the land, such as the Farnsworth House. But it became evident that the positions themselves—the house as detached from or united with the site—were interrelated; land and house, site and object would be constructed simultaneously.

The traditional house was conceptually a square with sides that held out the landscape. Through time, the square has evolved into an X that allows nature to work itself into the form. Eventually the X will also dissolve.

The relationship of the house to its site works from two directions, from the inside out and the outside in. From the inside out, the views are rigorously framed: up, down, or forward; close, far, or infinitely far. The site is both real and idealized, objective and subjective. From the outside in, the house sits on its own unfolded skin, both in and on the site but conceptually independent from it.

The land itself has also been shaped; the land is the skin of the earth. The house both marks and transforms this skin.

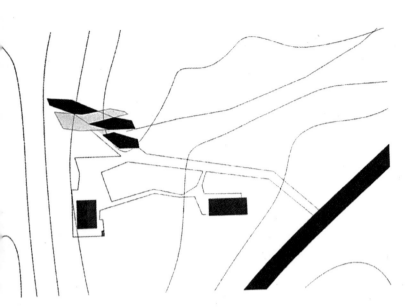

The millennium house articulates the relationship between the site, a plot of land in upstate New York, and a virtual historical landmark. The moment in time marked by the millennium and the millennial type pointed to an understanding of historicity different from both the tendency to reduce history to style (as an arbitrary visual convention) and the tendency to understand history as a material struggle beneath and beyond formalization.

Celtic Sun circles are an example of a structure that can function as an index, in this case, of the year 2000. Optical devices and time machines rearrange fragments of the landscape into topographical maps and inscribe them back onto the land. The earth is used both as "topic" of the construction, registering a fleeting moment on the surface, and as building material, indicating the repetitive potential of this transient instant.

SKINS AND SURFACES

Questions of enclosure came to the fore as the program began to be placed on the site. Skins and surfaces are tools of mediation between program and site, inside and outside, public and private, stasis and movement. At first, skins were assumed to be vertical, surfaces horizontal. But in reality, the architecture had to conflate and confound the horizontal and the vertical; the most important surfaces and skins were often those that pulled up from the ground and spiraled into the house. The house may be understood as a synthesis of surfaces and skins that register, through material or configuration, the forces of surrounding activities.

The enclosure for a house modeled on the interior space of the Dream House at the National Association of Home Builders Convention, should be as neutral as possible. The glass skin and truss structure evoke the manufactured nature of the image of "home."

The earth is not a solid but a series of layers; the top layer is geometricized and elevated to become the horizontal plane of the house. The earth's skin—artificial, cultivated, designed—is continuous with and indistinguishable from that of the house.

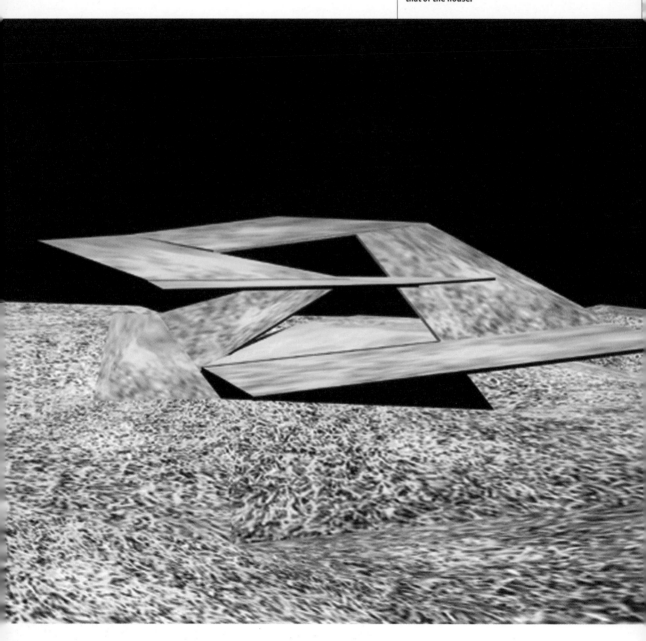

The topological/pleated/striated surface of the earth can perform the functions of structure, drainage, and lighting control. These traits phenomenologically and formally connect the building with the site.

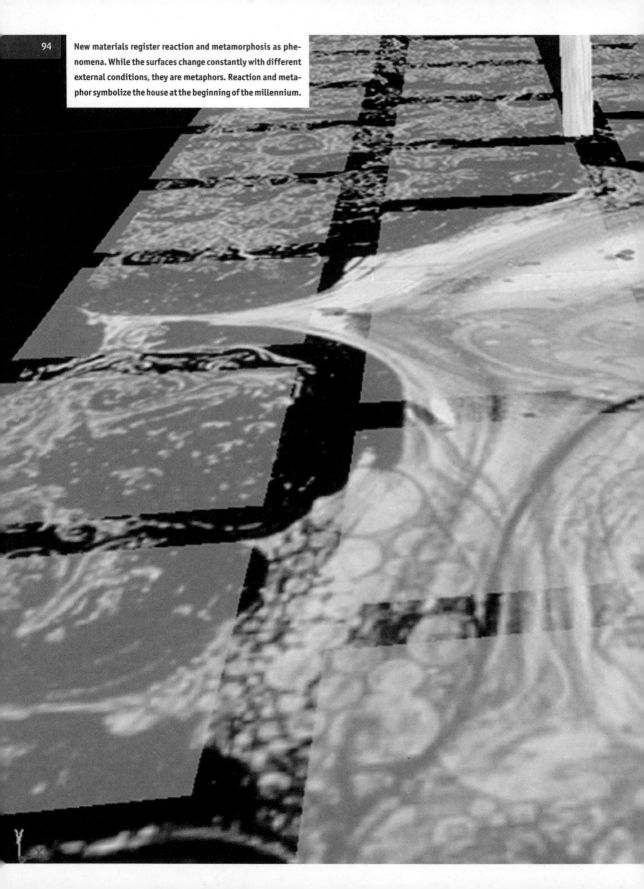

New materials register reaction and metamorphosis as phenomena. While the surfaces change constantly with different external conditions, they are metaphors. Reaction and metaphor symbolize the house at the beginning of the millennium.

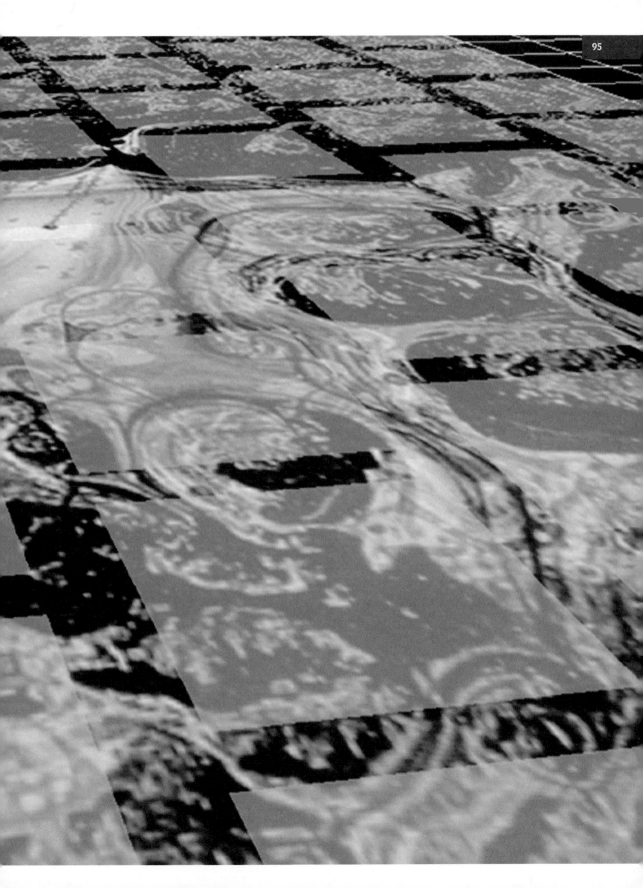

The outer wrapper and the inner tubes are differentiated but interlocked; they operate as a pair in relation to the occupants. The wrapper must be opaque so that the viewer cannot locate him- or herself through direct visual connection. The viewer's position in relation to the site should be ambiguous and complex.

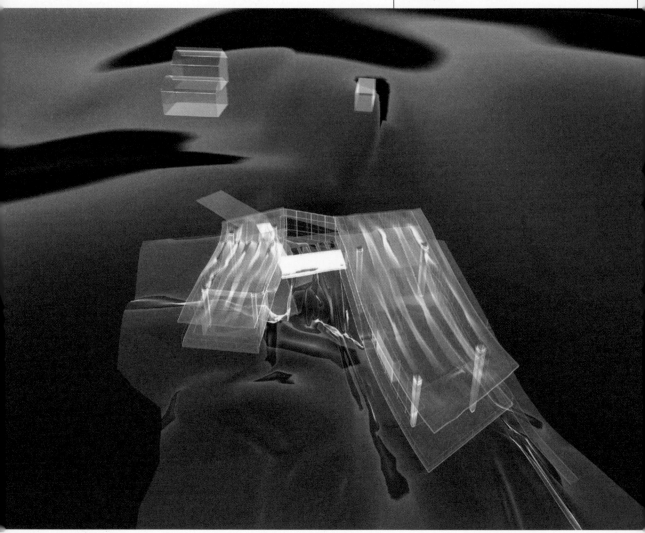

STANDARDIZATION AND MODULARITY

The studio discussed two potential outcomes of designing a hypothetical house: the one-off proposal, customized to fit the needs of a particular site and individual or family; a prototype that could lead to future housing variations. This issue is critical in the context of house-building in the United States. Commercial systems of design and construction are becoming so prevalent that the architect is removed from almost all domestic design. One ambition of the studio was to think beyond the typical high-end, elite approach to architecture (typical of academic studios and sometimes of the profession itself) to embrace and redirect house-building systems.

Room sizes have become indexes of luxury connected less to necessity and more to "comfort" and the good life. Today's master bathroom and kitchen balloon beyond the limits of functional requirements and enter realms of gigantism where square footage communicates more about a house than plans or photographs.

Programmatic relationships are absent from the display floor of the National Association of Home Builder's Convention. Rarely, and only coincidentally, do adjacent stalls evoke more than vague images of the industry's hierarchies and the exhibition's own bureaucratic organization.

A computer program could be developed to compete with an industry that is traditional in every aspect of its structure. The new software reconfigures the system on three levels—the formal, the social, and the technical. Formally, three enclosure methods use special effects and technology to create desire rather than historical re- or misappropriation. Socially, materials manifest themselves and attention is called to controlling devices—windows, frames, display of false wealth. Technically, new methods and materials are used to accomplish formal and social goals and to function in an environmentally responsible manner.

Completely Detailed Floor Plans

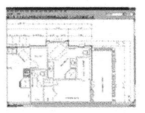

Automatic Generation of Cross Sections

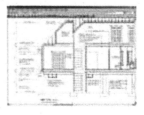

Automatic Generation of Elevations

ONE-OFF SYSTEM	GOAL	RESULT	# BUILT PER YEAR *
	A+	A+	1 unit
BUILDER SYSTEM	GOAL	RESULT	# BUILT PER YEAR *
	A+	F to C- consistantly	1.62 million units per year
NEW SYSTEM	GOAL	RESULT	# BUILT PER YEAR *
	A+	B -to B+ consistantly	1.62 million units per year

Complete Roof Layout and Framing Capabilities

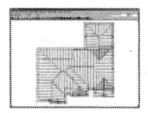

Complete Site Planning Utility

SOFTPLAN SYSTEM
(builder intuition based)

ORDER OF OPERATIONS

DRAW FLOORPLAN VIA ESTABLISHED WALL SECTION TYPE

DRAW INTERIOR PARTITIONS VIA ESTABLISHED WALL SECTION TYPE

ROOF GENERATED AUTOMATICALLY- ALTER IF NECESSARY

ADD WINDOWS FROM LIMITED PRE-PROGRAMMED TYPES

ADD DOORS FROM LIMITED PRE-PROGRAMMED TYPES

ENTIRE FRAMING AND ROOFING SYSTEMS ARE AUTOMATICALLY CALCULATED WITH DIMENSIONS AND PRICING

CHOOSE EXTERIOR CLADDING- PRICING IS AUTOMATICALLY GENERATED

ENTIRE COST OF BUILDING IS AUTOMATICALLY CALCULATED INCLUDING ALL PLUMBING FRAMING, SURFACING, INSULATION AND LABOR ACCORDING TO GEOGRAPHIC AREA

FULLY RENDERED VIEWS, AS WELL AS 3D FRAMING DIAGRAMS ARE AVAILABLE AT THIS POINT FOR MARKETING/ SALES

TOTAL TIME SPENT - LESS THAN 30 MINUTES

DIAGRAM GENERATED

NEW SYSTEM
(site/ user input based)

ORDER OF OPERATIONS

INPUT LOCATION PARAMETERS AND FINANCIAL LIMITATIONS

INPUT GENERAL ORIENTATION OF SITE/VIEWS AND SITE TOPOLOGY

INPUT SERVICES REQUIRED AND NUMBER OF OCCUPANTS

INPUT PREFERENCES IN LIFESTYLE TYPE

SEVERAL POSSIBLE OUTCOMES OF SITING, MASSING AND ORGANIZATION ARE GENERATED AS POSSIBILITIES THAT MATCH INPUT REQUIREMENTS

ALTER AS NECESSARY

VIEW RECOMMENDED CONSTRUCTION TECHNIQUES AND MATERIALS AVALIABLE FOR THAT REGION

ENTIRE COST OF BUILDING IS AUTOMATICALLY CALCULATED INCLUDING ALL PLUMBING FRAMING, SURFACING, INSULATION AND LABOR ACCORDING TO GEOGRAPHIC AREA

FULLY RENDERED VIEWS, AS WELL AS 3D FRAMING DIAGRAMS ARE AVAILABLE AT THIS POINT FOR MARKETING/ SALES

TOTAL TIME SPENT - LESS THAN 30 MINUTES

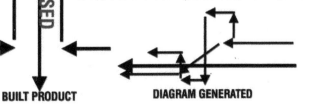

DIAGRAM GENERATED

ARTUR HOUSE

CURRENT INDUSTRY CONSTRUCTION SYSTEM USED

BUILT PRODUCT

In the same way that materials reinforce construction techniques, production techniques can change in relation to conceptual categories. The building shell, literally connected to the site, might employ standard techniques for on-site construction: poured-in-place concrete, on-site steel-frame fabrication, sheathing over structure. In contrast, production techniques for constructing functional tubes use a hybrid form of unibody frame construction (with current CNC milling techniques) along with a taut stressed skin. These methods differentiate between exterior and interior skins; while exterior skins would maintain a standard shape across different units, interior skins would modulate with the program. For example, private rooms need flat, level surfaces while lap pools do not. Such a double system of skins enables the manufacture of modular units that accept certain variation.

Interior Perspective "A" - Sketch

Interior Perspective "A"

Studio A

Lap Pool

Kitchen

Longitudinal Wall

Plan Sketch

Elevation Sketch

material x

Concrete Wall

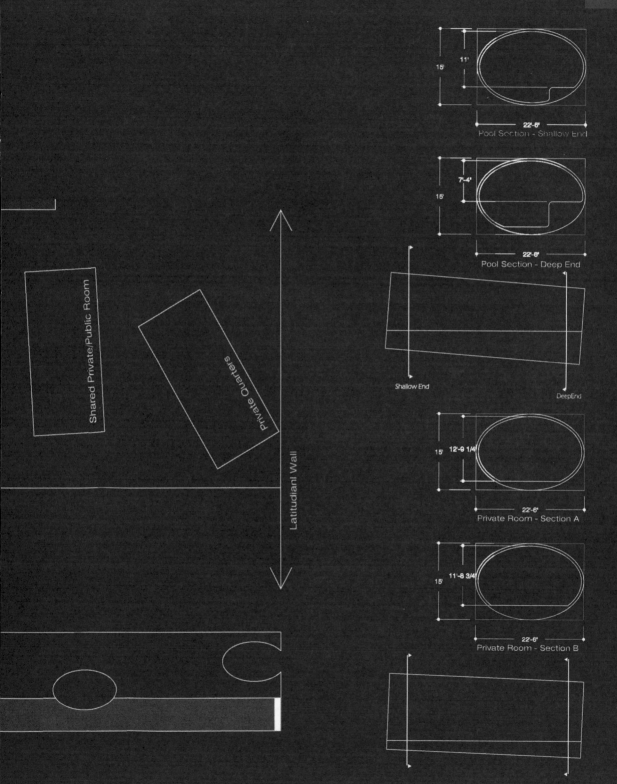

Pool Section - Shallow End

15'   11'   22'-6'

Pool Section - Deep End

7'-4'   15'   22'-6'

Shallow End   DeepEnd

Private Room - Section A

15'   12'-9 1/4'   22'-6'

Private Room - Section B

15'   11'-8 3/4'   22'-6'

Shared Private/Public Room

Private Quarters

Latitudianl Wall

Mark Wamble's Klip House is a model of prefabrication, standardization, and branding for future affordable production methods. Using shipping container technology in combination with this approach will engender greater varieties in spaces, sequences, and openings.

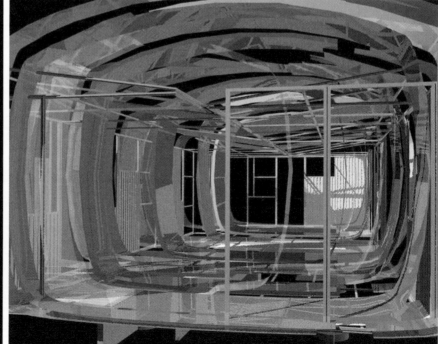

PLANS, PROGRAMS, AND POSSESSIONS

As the studio discovered in an analysis of the traditional image of house, traditional assumptions about program are open to reconsideration. Are typical rooms still necessary as functions blend or require flexibility? Are clients still primarily heterosexual couples? If not, does the nature of the "master bedroom" or "family room" change? Has modern technology provided a different type of leisure time? The plan by definition registers these changes. It should be seen not in terms of allotments of floor area but in terms of the activities and possessions of the owner. The movement, placement, and apparatus of the body must be studied in relation to each other and in relation to enclosure and site.

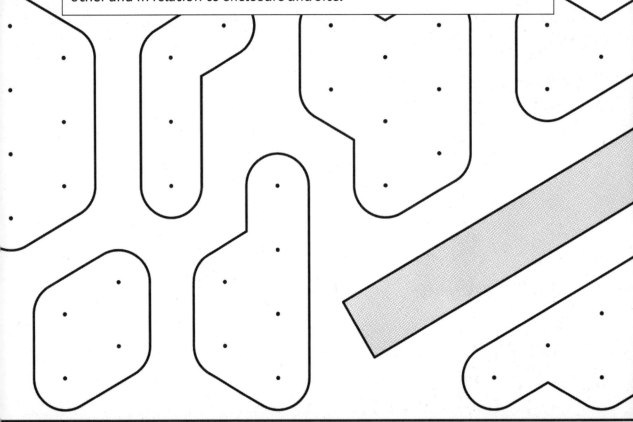

Abstract and nearly arbitrary rules define the house. A measurement of six feet, the length of the average electrical cord on home appliances, outlines zones such as the cooking area in a series of twelve-foot circles. The appliances themselves are laid out in alphabetical order. These rules project the notions of convenience, luxury, and normalcy.

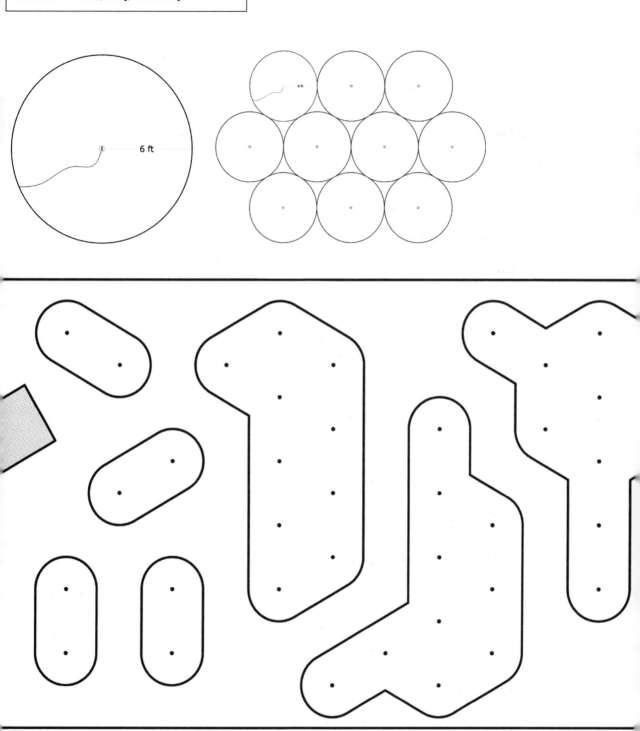

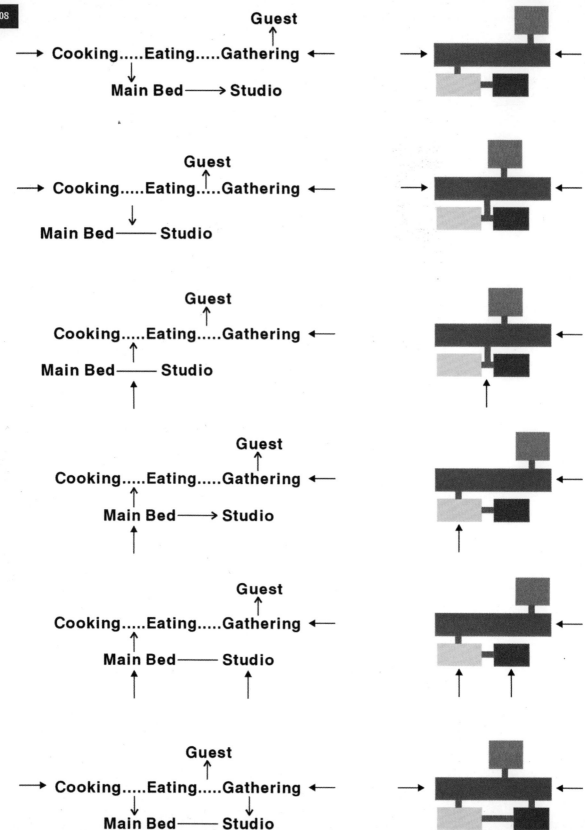

The location of equipment makes the plan more specific than one with rooms of specific functions. Flexibility localizes relationships of activity operating both beneath the house (site infrastructure) and in the house (domestic infrastructure).

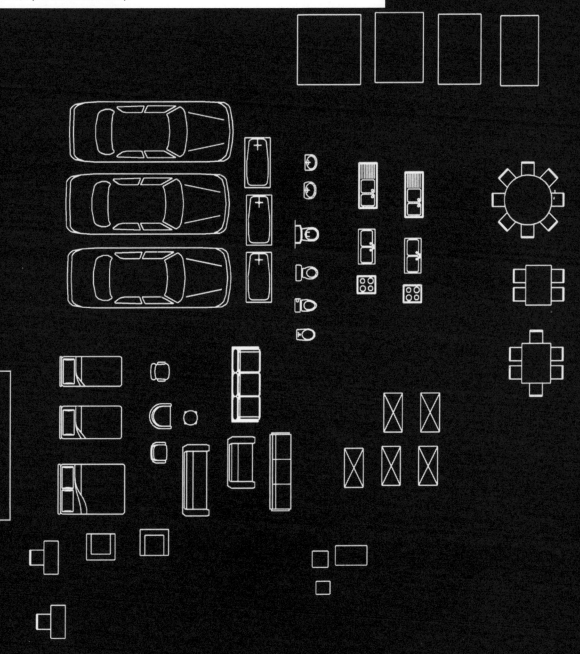

EQUIPMENT PATTERN

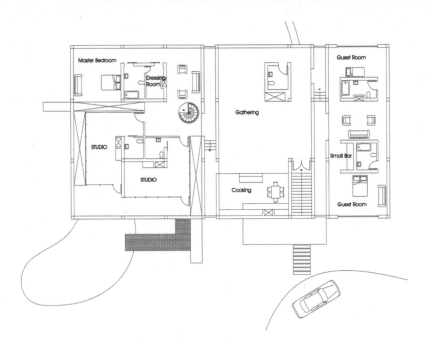

Master Bedroom

Dressing Room

Guest Room

STUDIO

Gathering

Small Bar

STUDIO

Cooking

Guest Room

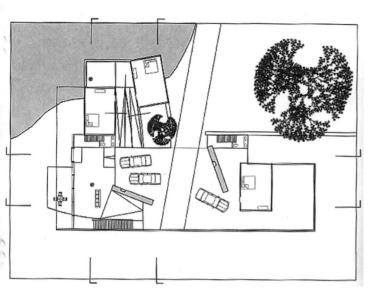

The scale of the landscape (roads and cars, barns and tractors), and the scale of the domestic program (road and hall, car and couch, tree and table, pool and tub) are physically collapsed in a single, continuous space.

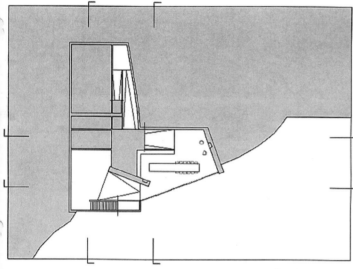

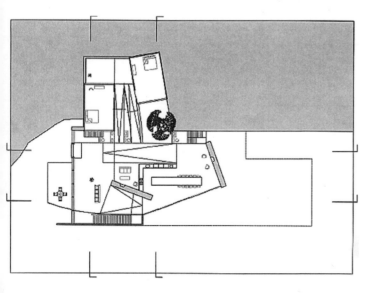

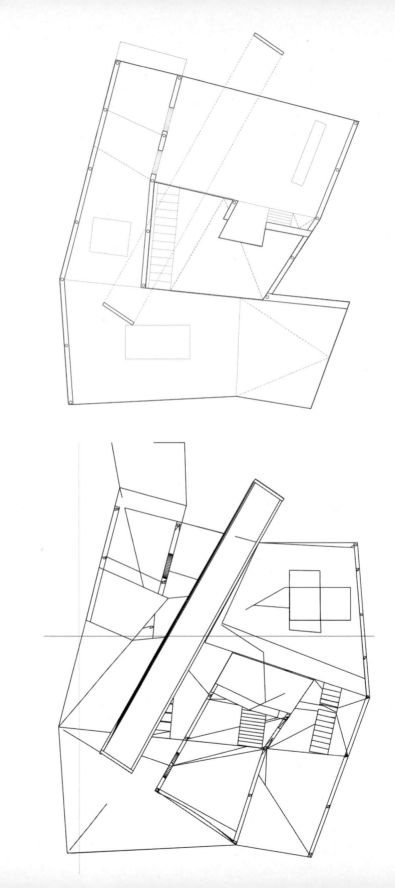

The plan puts the bedroom at the center, floating on water, while the edge contains peripheral activities distributed unhierarchically.

SECTION AND STRUCTURE

Section and structure implant a project at the intersection of surface, site, and body. Techniques of building that either expose the structure or embed it within the skins and surfaces of the house proved particularly relevant to the studio. While the section can typically expose the spatial hierarchy of a house, in this case, it was important to register the place of structure in the hierarchy as well.

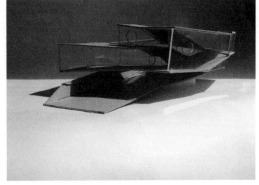

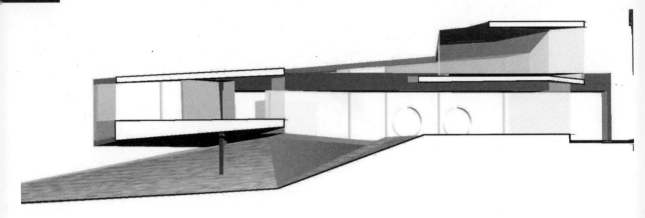

In section, indoor and outdoor spaces have equal value. They are thus physically and conceptually indistinguishable.

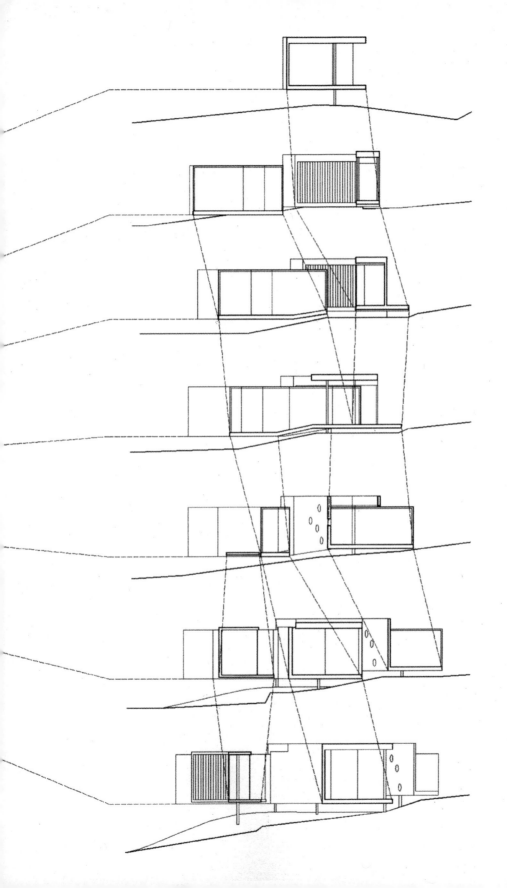

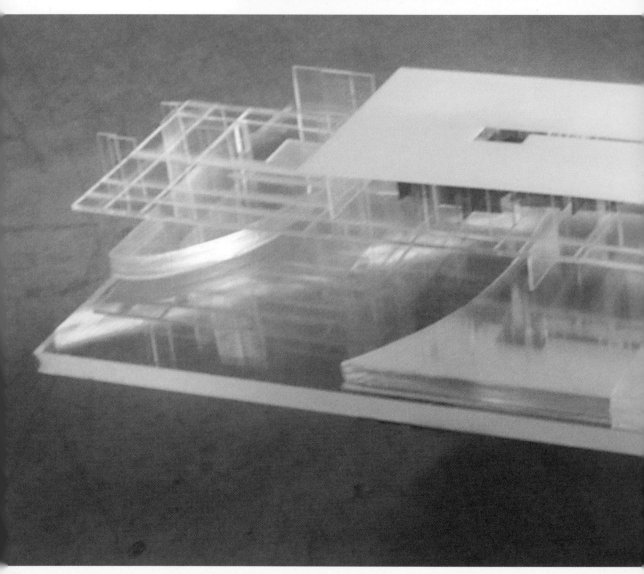

A series of sliding walls/doors determines the structure and the sections, dividing the house for multiple uses and freeing the plan. Sliding devices are carried to the elevations: walls/doors can be positioned to break down divisions between inside and out and even alter the appearance. Voids become solids and visa versa.

LIGHT AND THE PASSAGE OF TIME

Time can be measured in millennia, centuries, and decades, but also in the passage of seasons and hours. Experiential time, and the registration of it by varying qualities of light, must be part of any contemplation of the significance of building in the new millennium. As the studio's proposals attained a certain physicality, the ephemeral temporal conditions of the site presented another challenge. The vital influence of such site conditions is evident in projects that record changing light and moving shadows.

OCTOBER

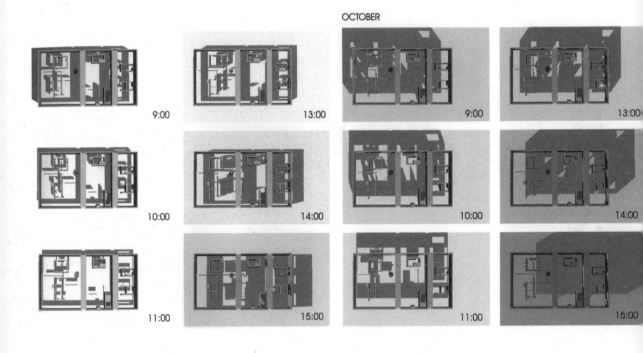

9:00

13:00

9:00

13:00

10:00

14:00

10:00

14:00

11:00

15:00

11:00

15:00

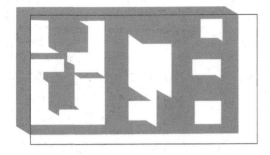

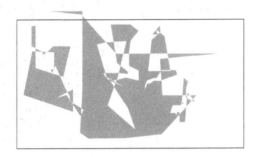
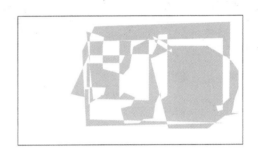
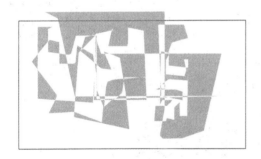

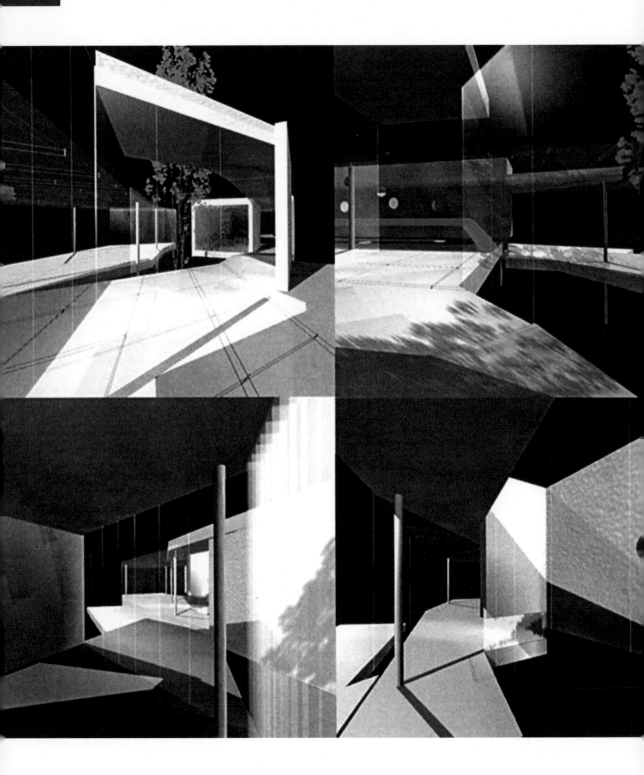

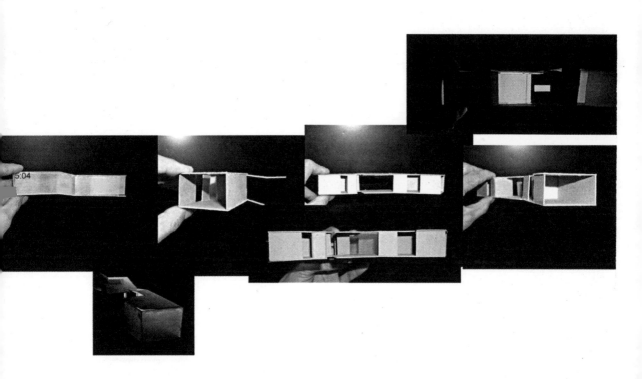

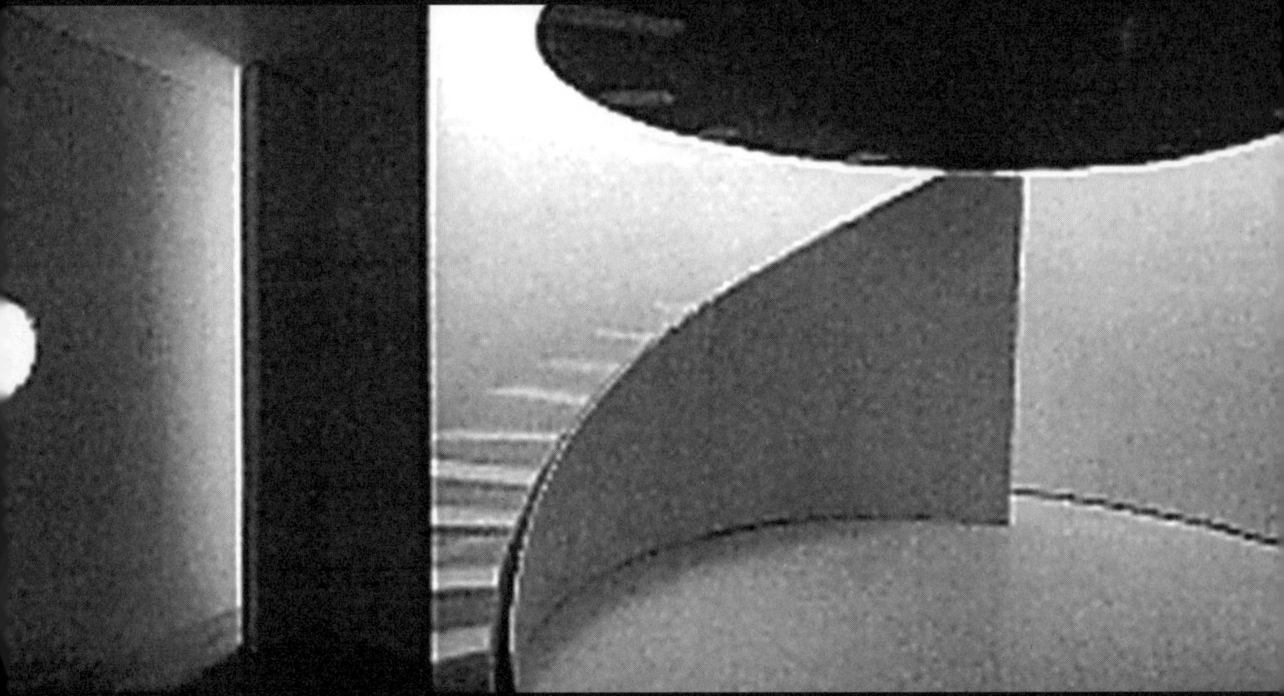

NETWORKS AND DIAGRAMS

Networking and diagramming are techniques that assist in situating a house in a larger context of internal domestic relationships. Such techniques are applicable to themes drawn from the consideration of program; many components of a house—appliances, computers, televisions, security systems, and the like, all controlled by local, regional, national, and international communications networks—have a role in orchestrating domestic activities according to the logic of a system. An analysis of networks and diagrams leads almost inexorably to an examination of the underlying organizational systems omnipresent in selecting places for objects, partitions, openings, and sequences.

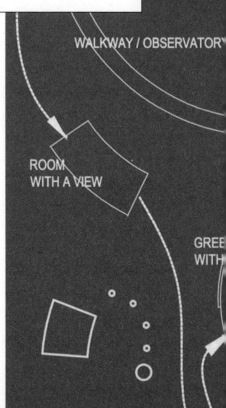

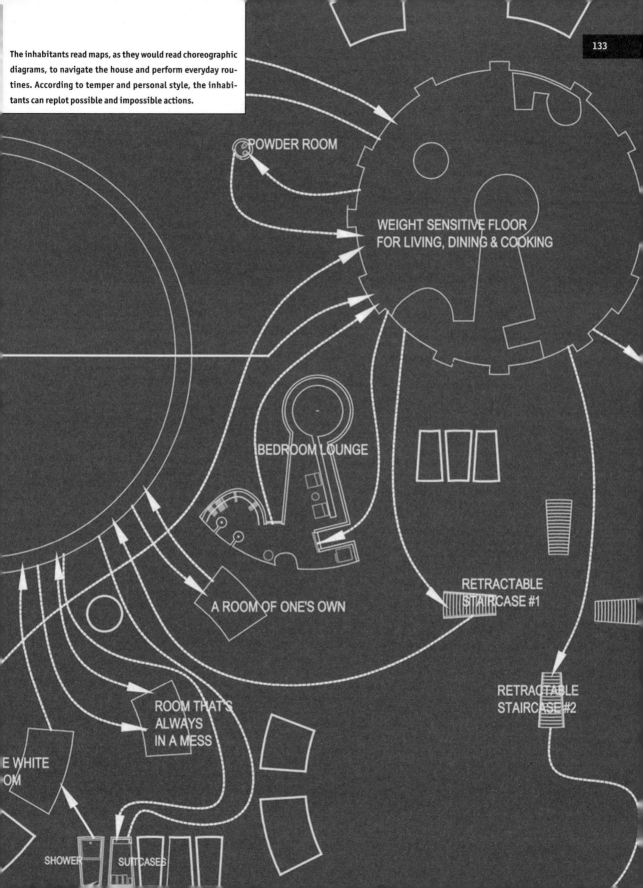

The inhabitants read maps, as they would read choreographic diagrams, to navigate the house and perform everyday routines. According to temper and personal style, the inhabitants can replot possible and impossible actions.

POWDER ROOM

WEIGHT SENSITIVE FLOOR
FOR LIVING, DINING & COOKING

BEDROOM LOUNGE

RETRACTABLE
STAIRCASE #1

A ROOM OF ONE'S OWN

RETRACTABLE
STAIRCASE #2

ROOM THAT'S
ALWAYS
IN A MESS

E WHITE
OM

SHOWER   SUITCASES

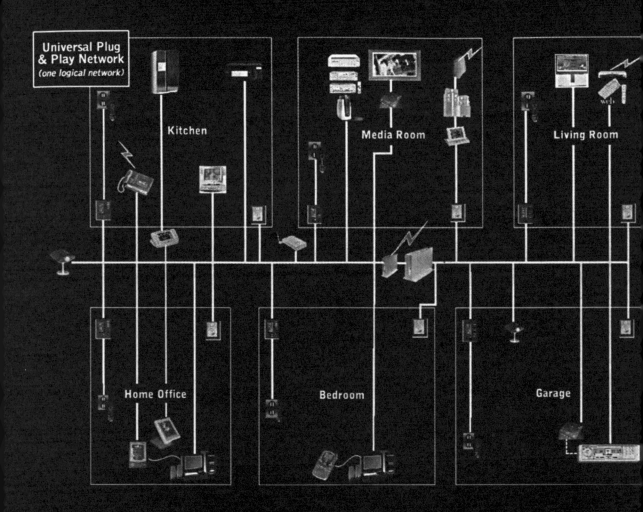

Universal Plug & Play Network
(one logical network)

Kitchen

Media Room

Living Room

Home Office

Bedroom

Garage

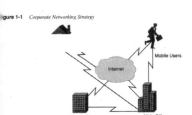

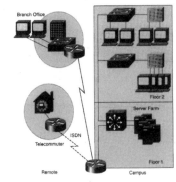

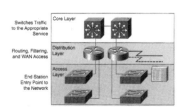

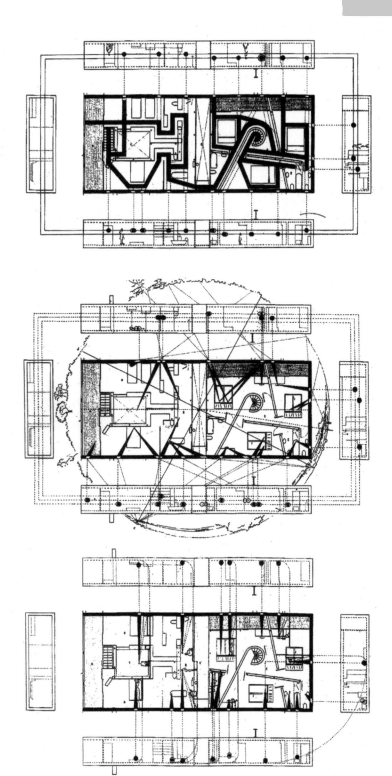

The corridor plan, designed to express persistence of vision, exemplifies the scopic control network. Images registered on the retinal surface persist for approximately $1/22$ of a second and are perceptually "stitching" together into a continuous whole. Sight lines and reasonable foveal ranges determine the window dimensions from a typical path down the corridor. Window width is uniform; the plane of the window openings is perpendicular to the sight line, making the shifting angle more overt. A range of 40 degrees is an approximation of the optimum field for viewing a flat plane such as a cinema screen or window, and the distance from the plane is correlated with the width of the plane.

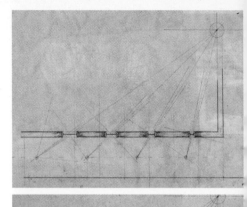

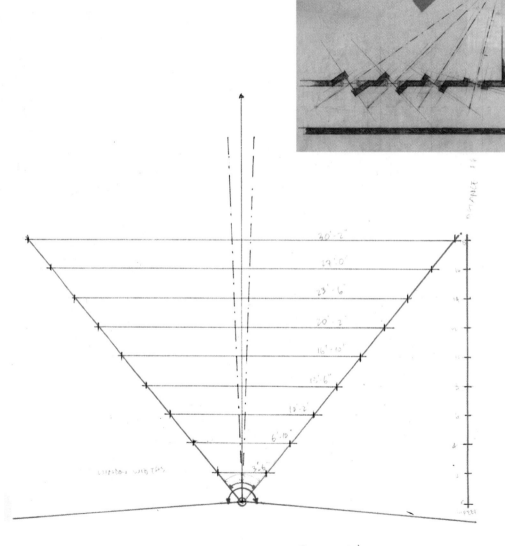

SCREENPLANE F.O.V. 80° (40°+40°)

MAX F.O.V. ⇒ 188° (94° + 94°)

¼ = 1'0"

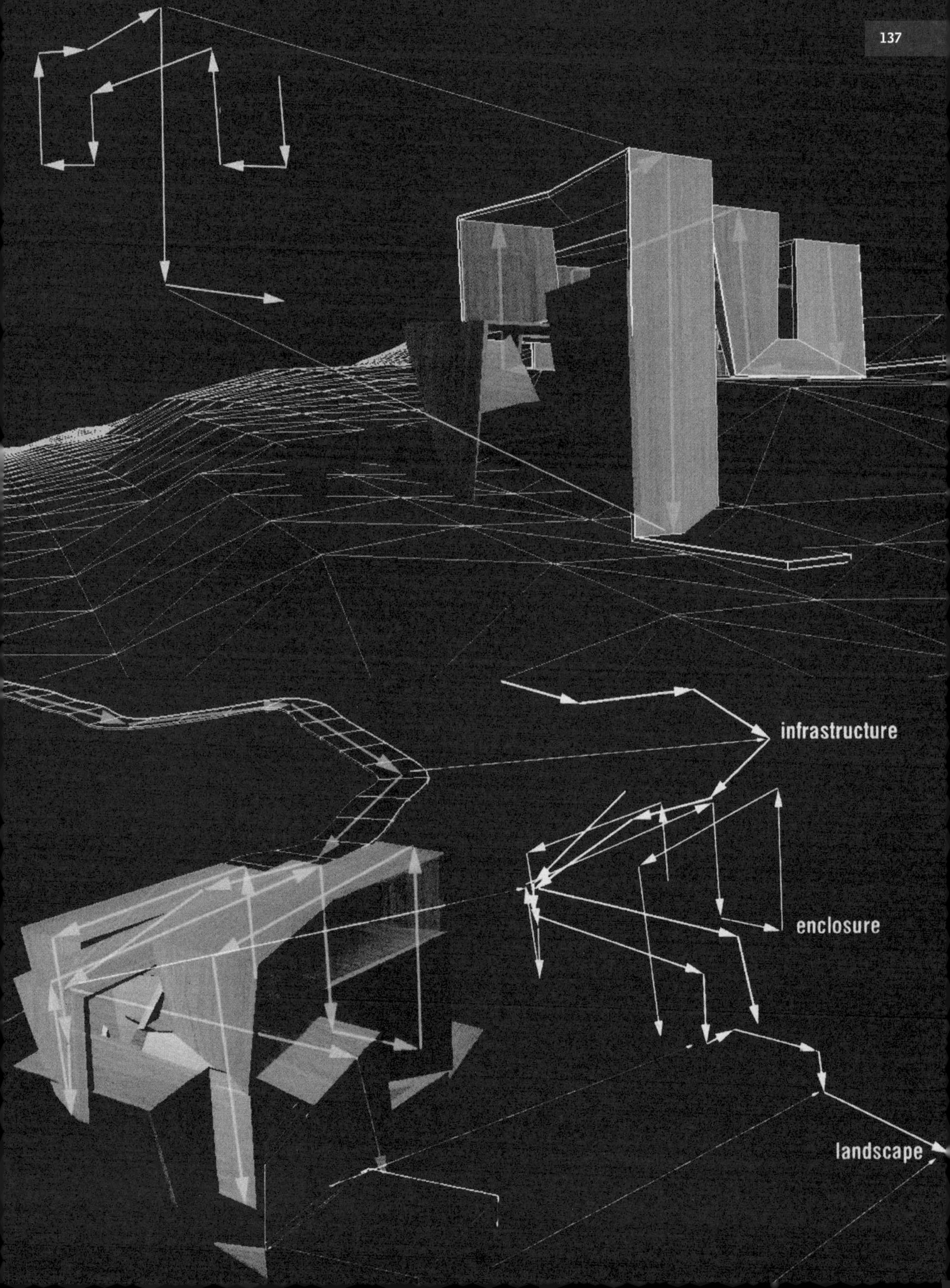

infrastructure

enclosure

landscape

SITE AS INFRASTRUCTURE

Just as an analysis of networks and diagrams clarifies the relationship between systems and plan, a consideration of infrastructure offers an opportunity to examine the site as a broader field of operations. In other words, landscape is not just "nature" but a system of codified roads, airwaves, electrical cables, phone wires, septic systems, and so on connecting one site with the next. As the studio had discovered, such an investigation is relevant not only to houses strongly integrated in the site but also to those detached from it. Houses are not just in/on the land, but in/on the grid.

Site, infrastructure, and house are conceived as a singular, continuous experience.

The house, at the top of a hill, is the culmination of the procession to it. Viewers can see their point of origin and their path at a different scale. The house both terminates and reopens the visual journey.

DETAILS AND MATERIALITY

Detailing, whether for a specific condition or as a more generalized component, unifies the physical aspects of a project and supports the relationships between house, body, and site. Details of joinery and assemblage allowed the studio to assess, on a small scale, concepts that had originated on a large scale. The attachment or detachment of surfaces and the choice of manual or factory assembly are relevant to both conceptual design and construction decisions. Product choices, for building and furnishing alike, are part of this assessment.

Products from the Home Builders Association Convention in Atlanta offered the home designer/shopper an expanded list of possible domestic material. As architects we might scorn the kitsch, however our design palette can be and was expanded and delighted.

ROCK
SPEAKER

thin transparent coated wires (1000x optical film)

dipped into transparent liquid plastic. **t**he plastic wetted - sticks to only parts of the surface covered by patterns of the wires. **a**fter plastic is solid - silver of the wires not covered removed by etching...

ice crystals (5x optical film)

glass, cold, water. . . formation.

damaged film (5000x optical film)

failure yields the unexpected and opens a new field. **i**ntended to provide the light for a flat panel display. **d**amaged during fabrication.

lichen (natural state)

moisture and dust - lichen extracts minerals from these as it grows: phosphates, sodium, potassium - microorganisms.

thin transparent coated wires (1000x optical film)

dipped into transparent liquid plastic. the plastic wetted - sticks to only parts of the surface covered by patterns of the wires. **a**fter plastic is solid - silver of the wires not covered removed by etching...

liquid crystal film (1000x optical glass/film)

liquid crystalline film is sandwiched between t electrical conductors: metallic film and a transp ent film of an electrically conducting metal oxi **w**hen an electrical potential is applied betwe these electrodes the molecules line up and li easily undulates through their loosely orde ranks; they are transparent and appear as b because a black (metal) backing shows throu **w**here there is no electrical potential the mo cules collect in groups - light passes through t changes course. result is white as the crystal film becomes milky and light scatters.

ferrofluid (10x optical film)

part liquid, part magnet (prepared - grinding magnetic lodestone - in an oil. grinding must be just enough). **m**ust not be so different in size from liquid (placed in magnetic field). **g**ravity, magnetism and surface tension shape the ferrofluid. magnets set within concrete surface. **w**hen sliding occurs image is created with the presence of light and optical plastic film onto the aluminum surface.

thin transparent coated wires (1000x opti

dipped into transparent liquid plastic. the plastic wetted - sticks to only parts of the surface covered by patterns of the wires. after plastic is solid - silver of the wires not covered removed by etching...

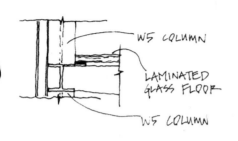

W5 COLUMN

LAMINATED
GLASS FLOOR

W5 COLUMN

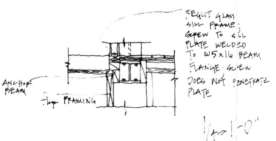

ANCHOR
BEAM

floor FRAMING

PLEXIT GLASS
SILL FRAME
SCREW TO SILL
PLATE WELDED
TO W5x16 BEAM
FLANGE GLEW
DOES NOT PENETRATE
PLATE

1/4" = 1'-0"

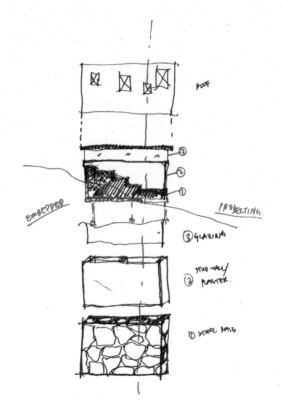

ROOF

EMBEDDED

PROJECTING

③ GLAZING

② STUD WALL PLASTER.

① STONE BASE

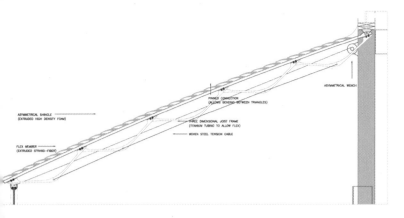

ASYMMETRICAL SHINGLE
(EXTRUDED HIGH DENSITY FOAM)

FLEX MEMBER
(EXTRUDED STRAND-FIBER)

PINNED CONNECTION
(ALLOWS BENDING BETWEEN TRIANGLES)

THREE DIMENSIONAL JOIST FRAME
(TITANIUM TUBING TO ALLOW FLEX)

WOVEN STEEL TENSION CABLE

ASYMMETRICAL WINCH

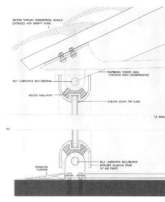

SECTION THROUGH ASYMMETRICAL SHINGLE
(EXTRUDED HIGH DENSITY FOAM)

SELF LUBRICATING BOLT/BEARING

MOLDED INSULATION

RESPONSIVE TENSION CABLE
(PREVENTS RAPID DECOMPRESSING)

CUSHION MOUNT FOR GLASS

1:2 SCALE

PERIMETER
FLASHING

SELF LUBRICATING BOLT/BEARING
EXTRUDED ALUMINUM FRAME
(AT END POINT)

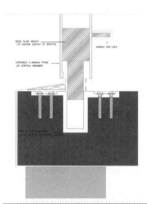

STEEL SLIDE WEIGHT
(TO CHANGE CENTER OF GRAVITY)

HANDLE AND LOCK

EXTRUDED ALUMINUM FRAME
(AT VERTICAL MEMBER)

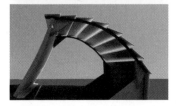

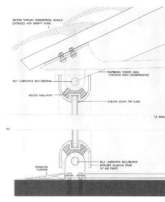

151

FINAL PROJECTS

The final product of the studio was a complete set of images—representations that exploited a never-to-be-built house. While formats varied widely, the intent was to present each project using graphic means that supported the project's essential qualities. In addition, students compiled their work in books, a more accommodating format. The audience for the projects was the review jury, not only the studio's "client." Nevertheless, the images needed to succeed not only as images but as the bearers of comprehensive information about a particular project, the Millennium House.

I AM THE AMERICAN DREAM

AM WASTEFUL OF MATERIALS, INEFFICIENT
N MY FUNCTIONING, AND I RELY ON THE
ESIRE TO IMPRESS AND CONTROL OTHERS
HROUGH THE ILLUSION OF WEALTH AND A
ALSE PARTICIPATION IN A HISTORY THAT IS
NYTHING BUT MY OWN

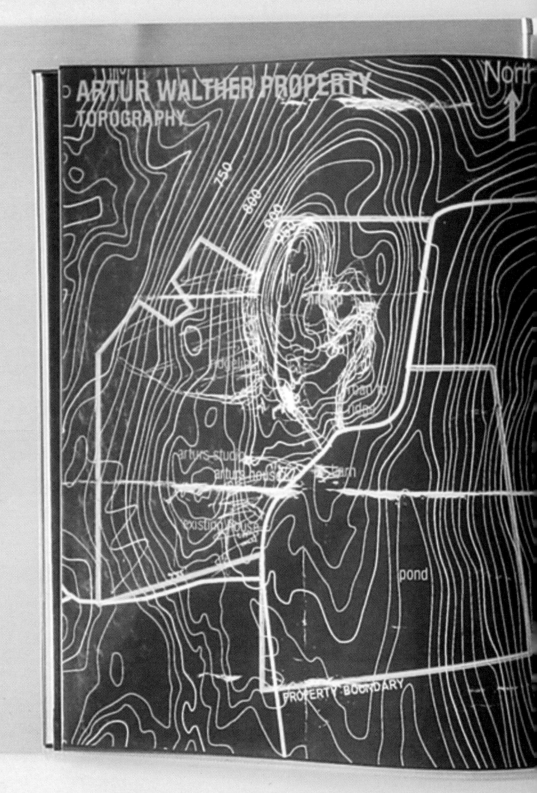

ARTUR WALTHER PROPERTY

ESTABLISHED VISUAL PILGRIMAGE ————————
PHYSICAL APPROACH ————————

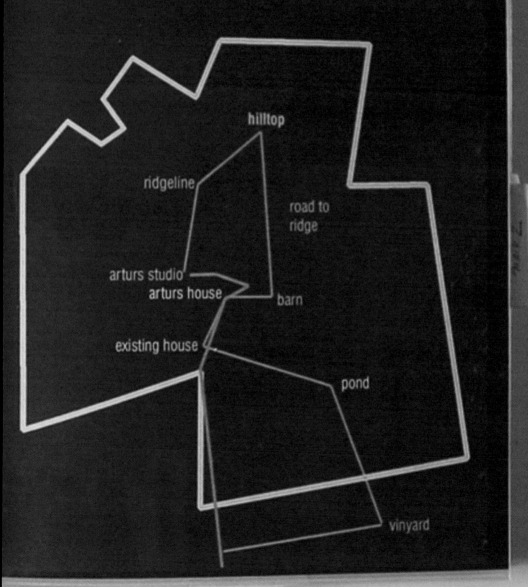

hilltop

ridgeline

road to ridge

arturs studio
arturs house

barn

existing house

pond

vinyard

Plans of Artur's House on Order

These other models of tatoos are available on order. They come 3.5", 2" and 1/2" sizes.

Model #2: Plan of Upper Floor

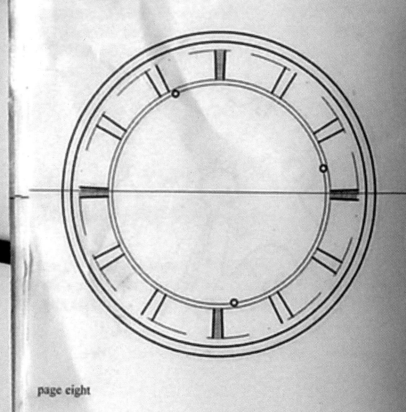

page eight

Model #3: Plan of Roof

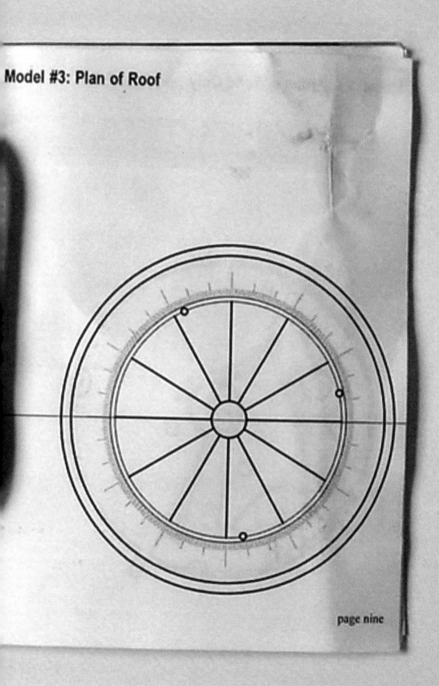

Model # 4: Arthur's World Only

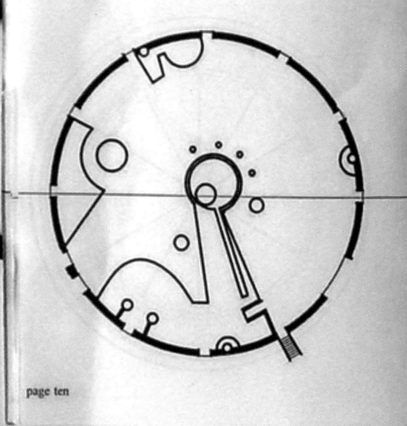

urface Viewer Locator

se the Surface Viewer Locator to locate light textures in the Surface
iewer as they appear in Artur's House (third millennium AD).

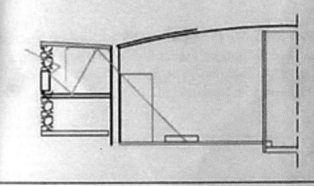

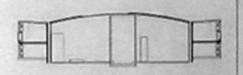

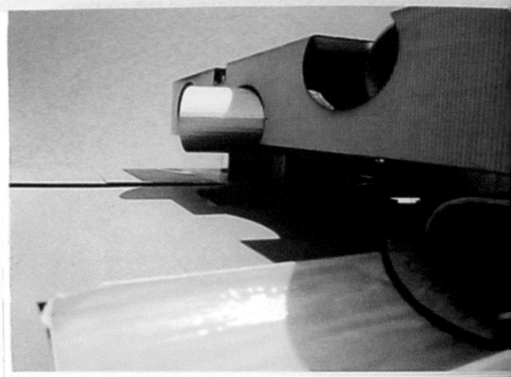

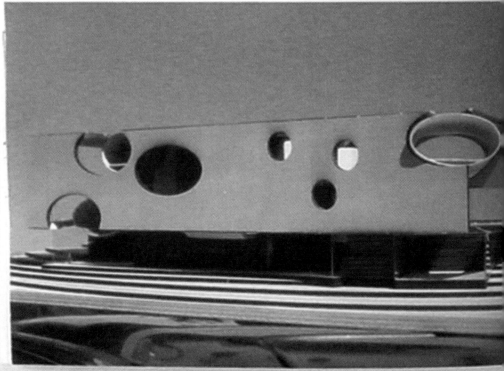

Clockwise from top left: View from lap pool looking towards kitchen tube; View down ramp towards entry court; Detail of private rooms- tube above, and room below; Rear facade 1/4":1' model - wood, wax, & plastic

Final Model Images- Millennium House (2001)

Intent: I understand these two parts - the outer shell and the inner tubes - as being engaged in dialogue, that is, they are differentiated but interlocked. They are operational as a pair in relation to their occupants. I do not consider these parts as being formally involved in a dialectic - i.e. I am not intending to resolve the tension between two different ideas, but rather, I intend to play off the tension between them; "truth" is not to be found in this synthesis, rather the perceptions of various subjects should render the house ambiguous, complex and [unresolved?]. For example, the opening in the outer shell are aligned for the direct views inside the rigators; however, views are bleed through to the (antispace?) enclosure below. Example 2: (From Eric) tubes that are fabricated for (subjective) views outside are themselves viewed as objects inside.

Observation: The extended walls on which the house was previously sited have become overpowered by the shell that poaches space. These walls, however, were only ever devices used to associate house part 'A' with the site (in distinction from house part 'B'). Instead, the exterior shell, used as a wrapper, may achieve this end through being embedded into the ground. The differentiation is then between part 'A' - attached to the site - and part 'B' - set on the site. This necessitates a third structure - mediation between the two.

Requirement: The wrapper needs to be opaque. A transparent shell would undermine a subject's ability to relate their position vis-`-vis part 'A', part 'B', and the landscape as ultimately incoherent. That is, being able to locate themselves through direct visual connections, it would be difficult for a viewer to render their situation ambiguous or complex.

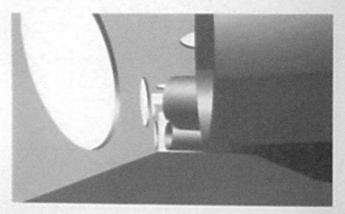

Top of page, left and right: Schematic model showing tubes, wrapper and structural wall (digital construction). Bottom of page, left and right: Concept model of tripart construction, folded skin (red) and tubes (yellow) with (blue) intermidiary. (colored craft paper).

(Bruce) Mau : Plans + Layouts

09/02

Figure 1-1 Corporate Networking Strategy

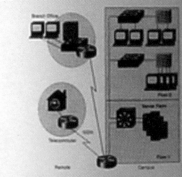

Figure 1-2 Group Interconnection

Figure 1-3 Three-Layer Hierarchical Network Model

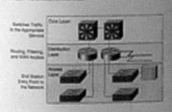

HOUSE
#X

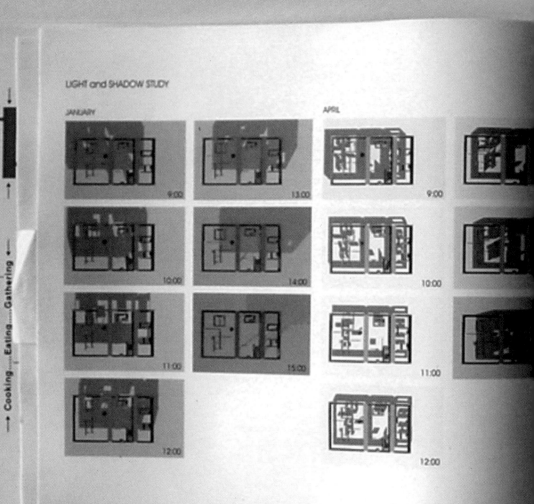

LIGHT and SHADOW STUDY

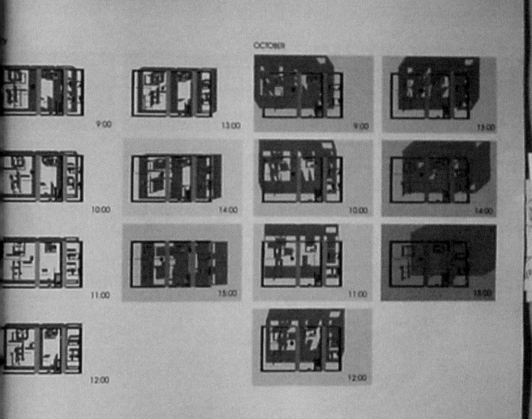

OCTOBER

9:00

10:00

11:00

12:00

13:00

14:00

15:00

9:00

10:00

11:00

12:00

13:00

14:00

15:00

Site Photos
S.01
Description:
View from SW
corner of property.
Process:
Digital photos
spliced and
cropped.

S.02
Description:
View from corner
of Earnest Rd. and
Hammond Rd. look-
ing NW.
Process:
Digital photos
spliced and
cropped.

S.03
Description:
Same as S.02 but
looking SE
Process:
Digital photos
spliced and
cropped.

Begin desk documentation/timeline. Develop light-study process for design. Beg
designing and building M.02.

04
Description:
View from Hammond
... over southern
section of prop-
erty.
Process:
digital photos
sliced and
cropped.

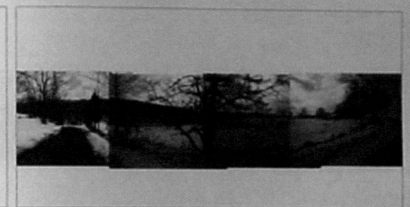

05
Description:
View from Hammond
... at a bend
looking SE
Process:
digital photos
sliced and
cropped.

06
Description:
View from NE
corner of site.
Process:
digital photos
sliced and
cropped.

M.01
Concept Model
Description:
A study model
exploring degrees
of exposure and
enclosure
Process:
Chipboard and
plastic with glued
joints.

M.01.A
Concept Model
Description:
Fully enclosed
quarter with two
blasted glass
walls. This room
would only allow
light and little
visual access in
or out.
Process:
Chipboard and
plastic with glued
joints then photo-
graphed and digi-
tally manipulated.

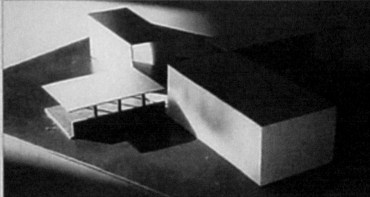

Page 6.

Begin designing first excercise, M.01. Formulate approach toward "image." Begin
designing book format. Photos not available.

1.B
ncept Model
cription:
tially enclosed
rter with one
sted glass wall
one clear.
room would
w light on
longer side and
ourage a framed
w of the land-
pe at the end.
cess:
pboard and
stic with glued
nts then photo-
phed and digi-
ly manipulated.

1.C
cept Model
cription:
ly exposed
rter with two
ss walls. This
m would allow
t and visual
ess in and out.
cess:
pboard and
stic with glued
nts then photo-
phed and digi-
ly manipulated.

1.D
cept Model
cription:
ly exposed
rter with no
sical enclo-
e. This outdoor
m is defined
y by low walls,
umns, and a
f.
cess:
pboard and
stic with glued
nts then photo-
phed and digi-
ly manipulated.

9/01   1/19/01   1/20/01   1/21/01   1/22/01

reaction and metamorphosis

movement - friction - change
constant - catalyst - product
concrete - metal - glass

looking southeast.

week 13 > **image revisited** > 04: 16 : 01

The fire was certainly the most life-like element of the house: it consumed food and left behind waste; was warm, one of the most fundamental qualities that we associate with our own lives. When the fire dies the concept of the soul that animates the physical body of the person, the fire, then, is the animating spirit

"i think everybody should be a machine"

ANDY WARHOL

>> week 9 >> **bodily objects** > 03 - 19 - 01

could grow and more seemingly by its own will; and it could exhaust itself and die. Most important it ts remains become very cold, just as the **BODY** becomes cold when a person dies. Drawing a parallel to or the body of the house.

-*Fire and Memory, On Architecture and Energy* Fernandez-Galiano/Carme

5:00 **X House** Yansong Ma
Yale Advanced Studio Spring 2000
Instructor: Peggy Deamer

How to Choose The Paths?   The X House Transforms Living in the House into a Walk in Nature.

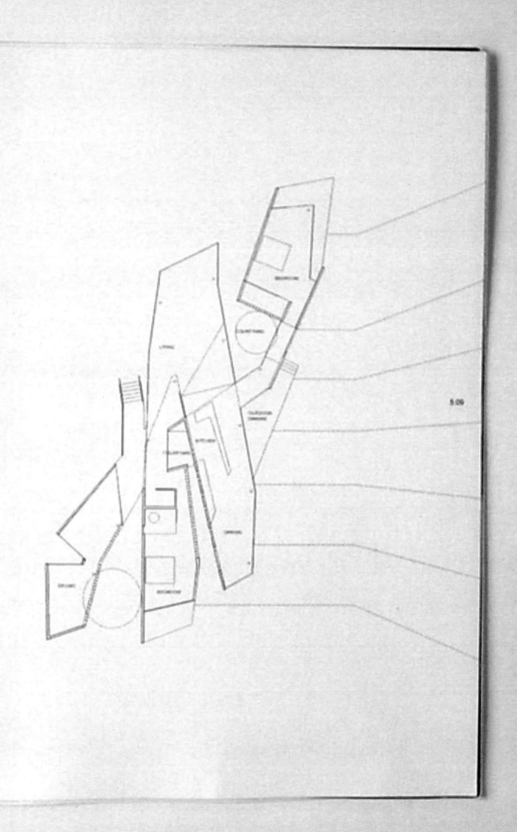

IMAGE REVISITED: REVIEWS

The studio returned to its first topic—image as an instrument to convey information—as part of the midterm and final reviews. Decisions relating to program, location, structure, and enclosure combined to create a metaphoric image of "house" and also a physical image with intent and aesthetic direction. Theories of representation, which may inform or seduce—or both—were addressed in relation to the potential client but also in relation to the review juries. Thus the reviews offered an audience for the studio's attempts to create an image of the Millennium House.

Andres Duany If you look at what has happened to architecture and materials, an idea of the Millennium House based on the dream house at the National Association of Home Builders might be considered a modern definition of "modern." It is interesting to look at what David Schwarz did for a new town in Texas. There he took all the classical buildings that he liked, put them in CAD, and sent them to a robot in Hollywood to make the elements. Modernism is about mass production and innovative materials, and you can harness it any way you need to.

Michael Bell One reason a dream house/Millennium House project might have a certain authority and force in production is that it puts the occupant in the powerful position. It is a useful place. The shell might be produced using contemporary building techniques and products— folded metal, Butler buildings, trusses, and expedient construction processes—but within there is a whole sustenance of the building tradition. Countering that crucible, the architect is in the position to choose how that will be interpreted and what will be encountered. A surrealist interpretation of sequences, for instance, would renounce authorship in favor of the next piece. A deconstruction of the production process can place the homeowner in a position of authority: the homeowner can witness how the house will get built before occupying it.

Robert A. M. Stern This is the far land that we dream about, where every man is his own architect. That is what is happening now. Whether it is the institutionalization of Home Depot or the capability of direct fabrication, the logic is provided by the restraints of life safety. It is like when people revolutionized sewing by cutting their own dresses or suits and making their own clothes with a Singer sewing machine. It reminds me of the Robert Venturi exhibition at the Corcoran Gallery of Art thirty years ago.

Leon Krier The industrialized home market is perverse, not because it is selling a product but because people are so alienated from the way they live, work, study, and have children that they have become completely anaesthetized to suffering. They drive through roads of garbage and they are alienated. Their first house is junk and their second house is junk. The way to contest the market is not by exposing it—everybody knows that it is junk— but by building a real house, not an alienated house in an alienated city.

Peggy Deamer One question is that of the container. Whether or not you like the technology, whether it is about material authenticity, it isn't about the arrangement of the interior but whether or not you want to expose arbitrariness. How do you want the container to display arbitrariness?

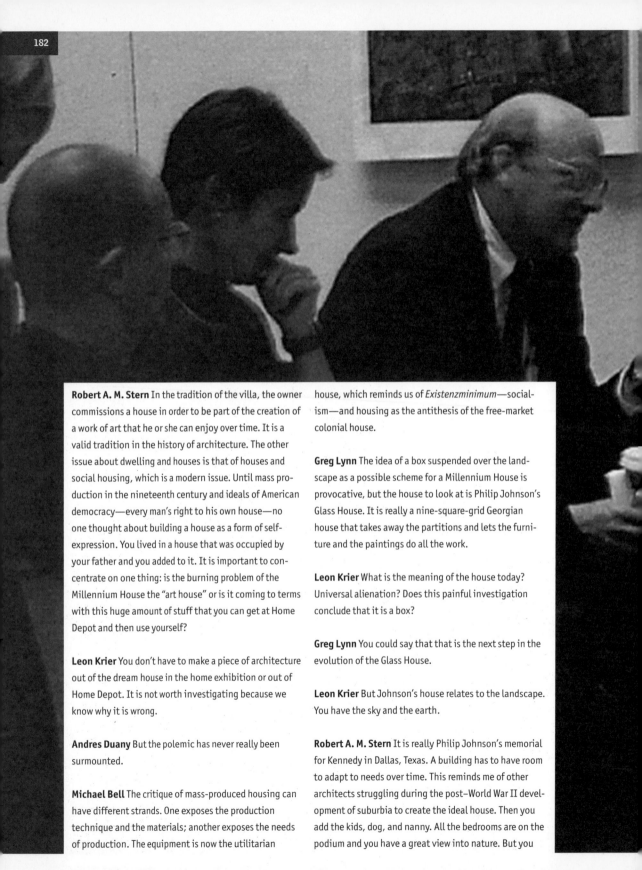

Robert A. M. Stern In the tradition of the villa, the owner commissions a house in order to be part of the creation of a work of art that he or she can enjoy over time. It is a valid tradition in the history of architecture. The other issue about dwelling and houses is that of houses and social housing, which is a modern issue. Until mass production in the nineteenth century and ideals of American democracy—every man's right to his own house—no one thought about building a house as a form of self-expression. You lived in a house that was occupied by your father and you added to it. It is important to concentrate on one thing: is the burning problem of the Millennium House the "art house" or is it coming to terms with this huge amount of stuff that you can get at Home Depot and then use yourself?

Leon Krier You don't have to make a piece of architecture out of the dream house in the home exhibition or out of Home Depot. It is not worth investigating because we know why it is wrong.

Andres Duany But the polemic has never really been surmounted.

Michael Bell The critique of mass-produced housing can have different strands. One exposes the production technique and the materials; another exposes the needs of production. The equipment is now the utilitarian

house, which reminds us of *Existenzminimum*—social-ism—and housing as the antithesis of the free-market colonial house.

Greg Lynn The idea of a box suspended over the landscape as a possible scheme for a Millennium House is provocative, but the house to look at is Philip Johnson's Glass House. It is really a nine-square-grid Georgian house that takes away the partitions and lets the furniture and the paintings do all the work.

Leon Krier What is the meaning of the house today? Universal alienation? Does this painful investigation conclude that it is a box?

Greg Lynn You could say that that is the next step in the evolution of the Glass House.

Leon Krier But Johnson's house relates to the landscape. You have the sky and the earth.

Robert A. M. Stern It is really Philip Johnson's memorial for Kennedy in Dallas, Texas. A building has to have room to adapt to needs over time. This reminds me of other architects struggling during the post–World War II development of suburbia to create the ideal house. Then you add the kids, dog, and nanny. All the bedrooms are on the podium and you have a great view into nature. But you

are compromising the ideal—maybe that is what the house is about.

Michael Bell It is a question of the house in relationship to territory. If you are trying to reveal or eradicate the networks that link it back to utilities and other companies, then the ultimate motif is that the architecture is the skin that separates the body from the earth, one nervous system from the other. How effectively can you do that? The argument is pivotal. The family, which Johnson put downstairs, comes back to the house.

Andres Duany If you have solid walls, nature will die, and you will have to replace it with artificial nature, consumptive of nature. You could have a mushroom patch and it would be changed by your intervention. Trees need sixteen square feet to thrive. There is so much false nature now. Nature might have to be replicated.

Thomas Phifer But something else could go on there with, let's say, water.

Peggy Deamer But in some way there is a question of real versus pure nature, which talks about the comings and goings of the house and the use of the land, because it is part of a larger economic system.

Greg Lynn When architects evoke nature it is for aesthetic and atmospheric reasons, not preservation reasons. Preindustrial nature doesn't exist because we are so involved in nature. But we master it too, with inventions like glow-in-the-dark chartreuse dogs. You have to have some design motivation.

Michael Bell On the one hand, the Millennium House is a serious project as a commission, and on the other, it is about the globalization of wealth and the return to a pastoral relationship with the landscape. To put that in the middle of an architecture school is a problematic situation. You are dealing with a level of irony—the car coming into the house, the water flooding in. One way around it is by touching the ground lightly—an authentic proposition. It has been a while since we have been concerned with touching the ground lightly.

Andres Duany We used to design quite large, expensive houses for clients, but we couldn't get interested in the clients' little narratives. And you noticed that our practice collapsed. We haven't done an expensive house for ten years because clients know that we don't really care about them. The last house we did was so grotesquely expensive that the only way I could conceive of it was by thinking that after the "revolution" it would be the people's yacht club. It is actually not so unusual. After people die or lose their fortunes the house can turn into something else.

Tom Phifer How does research in materiality influence the more formal properties of a house and a parti? How does it affect the view and the siting?

Greg Lynn You have to talk about precedent. There are various provocative directions to take in material research. One way is to approach the Millennium House as an encyclopedic cabinet, using it for a grid of material properties to store all the elements as a sample. The "sample" could itself be used as a building material in a way that limits a lot of the pattern. Or there could be an Art Nouveau strategy where pattern and material work with surfaces and provide a new approach to vegetable form that is not just decorative pattern but structure—hand rails, appliances, light fixtures. What is most interesting in these patterns is not the visual effect but the way they work with a boundary condition or a surface. The way a crystal forms and articulates edge, center, and pattern is more effective than photocopying it and sticking it onto a surface. But it also requires a sophisticated design technique. A third way would be to make it, as Herzog & de Meuron or Warhol would, into a kind of decal.

Tom Phifer If that idea is taken one more step, the HVAC and wiring services could be integrated with the structural systems. But sooner or later the house would have to become site specific, and usually these things come together at one time. You can do wonderful research to find what is appropriate spatially, how you choreograph getting there, how it is oriented and ventilated—and you converge all this research together with an actual idea about how to make a house. How are you actually going to apply this to the site to make it specific? How will you respond to the light? Spectacular painters have been painting this landscape for decades. You could have studies of light in different seasons and how light reflects off snow, grass, and trees to get really site specific. This is a conscientious effort to see what light can do with a contemporary understanding of technology and materials, which then goes back to the site and nature.

Michael Bell I am linking the word memory to Bergson, Rossi, and architecture or philosophy, where memory is understood as catalytic or chemical based, so it stops being about figuration or mysticism and becomes gray matter. You compress vision and materials at the molecular level and then you can reset the horizon. Greg's version is interesting in terms of production techniques; Herzog's version pushes the limits of the box. There is a buildable consequence of working at a molecular level. The horizon of Albert Bierstadt and others is linked to this molecular horizon. The revolutions of the twentieth century are molecular. In some ways the scientific revolutions are already there in the house—the freon in the refrigerator, the silicon seal. How do you unhinge the materials into the space and recalibrate the volume?

Paul Lewis One idea for a Millennium House might have no two rooms the same; it is the test-tube analogy and the building. And then it changes at different scales. It is interesting to make two rooms that are never the same architecturally and flip that around by asking, how does that influence the nature of the house in a more speculative way?

Greg Lynn Here is a more severe diagnosis. Silk screening is a technique of Herzog & de Meuron, Warhol, and Rauschenberg. They were looking for certain effects, and there was a technology that would allow them to explore those effects. This research could be about the subdivision of space based on pattern, or temperature zones, or gradients of light and enclosure. Rooms and zones could be distributed with these kinds of techniques. For example, you could locate rooms with chemical research the way Frei Otto did.

Michael Bell The house is a commodity now, produced by benchmark standards of efficiency and shrinking profit margins, like any commodity. One way to gain efficiency is to find a way to produce it with infrastructure. There is a benchmark level of efficiency in industry, which means there will be a profit, but when everyone else reaches that level, the profitability is lost. It is a never-ending game.

Andres Duany It works the other way around, too. When lower benchmarks are set, everything gravitates down. There used to be many window companies in Miami. Now there is one miserable one that is cheaper, and every manufacturer is lowered to that level.

Michael Bell I understand why that would be the supposition. You wonder why you should compete with a vigorous system where the next level of innovation would make it a commodity.

Leon Krier The existing system may be alienated, perverted, and kitsch, but it talks to the large mass of the buyers' market. I think you can invent one new system that can blast that away. Architects have not been able to produce one house to replace the traditional house, not even Frank Lloyd Wright. Why don't you think in another way? Why don't you try to improve a system, rather than replace it, and make a really beautiful house?

Andres Duany You could use vinyl siding and make it a great system. And Dryvit has both enabled and destroyed postmodernism. It is the most modern and flexible material, but there is an inability to engage what can truly be used to build.

Greg Lynn It used to be that the auto industry designed a few cars of which they produced a few million. Now there is an explosion of models and styles just as with houses,

so that instead of 1.6 million colonials, you want to produce, deliver, and ship one thousand of them—you want to slot them into the model of car production. Maybe if you begin with ten a year, then one hundred, it is not exploiting the system.

Andres Duany In terms of production you could change all of the negative and the kitsch, but architects are not engaging the industry on its own terms. Why can't architects work with vinyl siding? Companies are bankrupt for ideas—you need to engage them. Someone came into my office with old tires. How do you make something with tires? Why aren't architects engaging the reality of production? The construction industry is bankrupt intellectually, and you can engage them by doing the next thing.

Leon Krier There is a profound desire to reinvent the house, which comes from a deep frustration that the house can't do what it is supposed to do. It has to do with how you read contemporary architecture. If you look at the way the piano and the violin developed and their various shapes—I have been looking for the one I want—the sound is fantastic, but the legs are not. Changing the house is a hopeless search, because the house has already been invented. It is still possible today to satisfy ambitions with traditional solutions. If you go into an experimental phase you need to have a very precise program—if you want to fly high or low—or

you end up in so many directions. It might be interesting, and it certainly doesn't challenge the idea of the traditional house.

Peggy Deamer You seem to be saying that there shouldn't be a challenge to the traditional house, and that in any case students are not the ones to meet the challenge. But I disagree with this. The real issue is, it is not an urban or economic problem. The Millennium House is a moveable target, and the students are solving a problem at the same time they are identifying it.

Andres Duany There is an absence of sociological and ecological concerns. What would have happened in a similar studio twenty-five years ago? Someone would have come with a knapsack and said, "This is the house." We would have applauded it. But there would have been someone else who would come up with a simple calculation saying this is a seven-million-dollar house, which could buy twenty-one vacation cottages and could be occupied at times by this person's friends and at other times by New York City kids. It would be an example of social equity completely outside the current box. The current box is completely circumscribed by high art and not by a true social engagement, and that is what is so radically different outside of studio walls.

Michael Bell The house is the last resort of subjectivity,

and it has been polarized between students and architects. Michael Hays in *Architecture* magazine said that architecture, as a retreat into narcissism, was trying to delineate subjectivity; it was trying to find out what it was "other" to. The more you delimit what architecture can't do, you find out what the real problems are. I think a lot of the problems today hit that.

Leon Krier But in this studio there were no luxurious houses with dancing halls and salons.

Michael Bell This is critical architecture.

Leon Krier Does that mean it is not splendid?

Michael Bell One thing you realize is that the house is a commodity. You wonder how it is produced and what the critical architecture is, and if you come at architecture from a critical position, you assume that there is something to criticize, and you probably assume and realize that architecture is more powerful than you are. And you have to get into it to change the gears. There is a hard psychological edge where housing is constructed by all of the mechanisms to extract profit, and where those things go together creates a milieu.

Leon Krier There is nothing wrong with designing an expensive house.

Michael Bell Are you separating beauty from politics?

Peggy Deamer It is a condition. The millennial is related to social and economic conditions, which have to do with the haves having more of the pie and the have-nots less. There is something about the notion of the weekend house and engaging with nature, but the client is not going to chop down a tree. To go to the country for the weekend in this day and age is so different, so luxurious.

Michael Bell You don't pick social and political agendas head-on, but look at the dream house from the Association of Home Builders convention. You can see in all the communities around Houston the huge level of psychological damage that instant houses inflict in the suburbs. But my optimism is the degree to which the house is still a site of experimentation and the degree to which in surrogate ways it can solve social problems.

Leon Krier The large country house—potentially . . .

Michael Bell It doesn't really exist in America. It is the Ralph Lauren ad.

Leon Krier The English country house is constantly a place to meet; there is a network of society.

Michael Bell But if you look at it as a commodity, if you

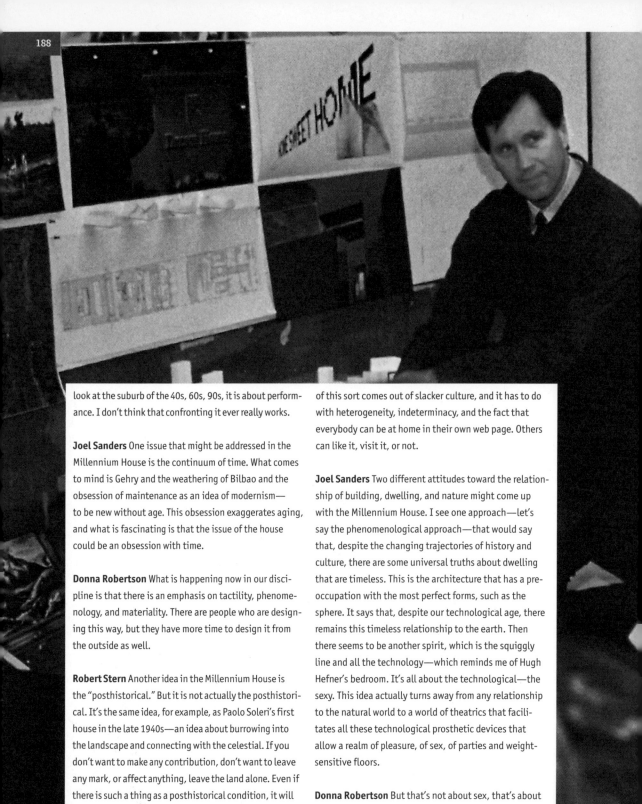

look at the suburb of the 40s, 60s, 90s, it is about performance. I don't think that confronting it ever really works.

Joel Sanders One issue that might be addressed in the Millennium House is the continuum of time. What comes to mind is Gehry and the weathering of Bilbao and the obsession of maintenance as an idea of modernism— to be new without age. This obsession exaggerates aging, and what is fascinating is that the issue of the house could be an obsession with time.

Donna Robertson What is happening now in our discipline is that there is an emphasis on tactility, phenomenology, and materiality. There are people who are designing this way, but they have more time to design it from the outside as well.

Robert Stern Another idea in the Millennium House is the "posthistorical." But it is not actually the posthistorical. It's the same idea, for example, as Paolo Soleri's first house in the late 1940s—an idea about burrowing into the landscape and connecting with the celestial. If you don't want to make any contribution, don't want to leave any mark, or affect anything, leave the land alone. Even if there is such a thing as a posthistorical condition, it will become history. All isms become wasms—immediately.

Donna Robertson I would say that a millennial condition

of this sort comes out of slacker culture, and it has to do with heterogeneity, indeterminacy, and the fact that everybody can be at home in their own web page. Others can like it, visit it, or not.

Joel Sanders Two different attitudes toward the relationship of building, dwelling, and nature might come up with the Millennium House. I see one approach—let's say the phenomenological approach—that would say that, despite the changing trajectories of history and culture, there are some universal truths about dwelling that are timeless. This is the architecture that has a preoccupation with the most perfect forms, such as the sphere. It says that, despite our technological age, there remains this timeless relationship to the earth. Then there seems to be another spirit, which is the squiggly line and all the technology—which reminds me of Hugh Hefner's bedroom. It's all about the technological—the sexy. This idea actually turns away from any relationship to the natural world to a world of theatrics that facilitates all these technological prosthetic devices that allow a realm of pleasure, of sex, of parties and weight-sensitive floors.

Donna Robertson But that's not about sex, that's about solipsism.

Tom Beeby The thing that's somewhat disturbing is this

trivialization of profound human activity. Isn't that a problem?

Joel Sanders I'm just posing it as two oppositions. It would be interesting to talk about how the natural and the cultural are imbricated.

Deborah Berke In the investigation of a circulation system through a house, it needs to be noted that how we live is not a direct path but a series of scattered shots—a line of movement doesn't describe our day.

Helene Furjan If you think about two sets of circulation as wrapping, with a membrane between them, how has landscape been reconfigured? How were country houses about landscape? Many nineteenth-century British houses are precisely about the building framing the landscape and the view out.

Joel Sanders I am interested in something more specific. A house organized around a driveway makes me think of the Villa Savoye, which is organized by the turning radius of the car. You have to stop and park and open a door. Then there is a ramp, which is disengaged from the landscape. If you are reconfiguring what that tradition seems to be about, you are reconfiguring the status of the automobile in the house. Then I think of the suburban house, which is organized around the entry and the front door. In developer homes, the new front door is the back door and the mud room; the plan is about packages coming in and specific ideas of everyday life. In a project with the car as the icon and focus of the house, even speeds of circulation can orient the space. What about speed and other circulation systems?

Donna Robertson You have to look at where we are in terms of the end of the last century and think about the idea of another middle landscape position: something between the natural and the artificial. That is what you mean by circulating in and then up and then through. You could take it to a condition of scalelessness. What differentiates the markers between this century and the twentieth century? How do those conditions therefore create an interior environment, a way of living?

Pages 16–17
Charles and Ray Eames, Eames House, 1945–49

Pages 18–21
Bernard Cache, Philibert de l'Orme Pavilion, 2000

Pages 22–24
Steven Holl, Simmons Hall, Massachusetts Institute of Technology, Cambridge, Massachusetts, 2002

Page 25
Steven Holl, Y-House, Catskill Mountains, 1999

Page 26
Kolatan/MacDonald, Meta Hom, Virgina, 2002

Page 28
Kolatan/MacDonald, Ha House, New York City, 2002

Kolatan/MacDonald, Raybould House and Garden, New York, 2002

Page 33
Garofalo Architects, Goszcycki House, 2001
Garofalo Architects, Manilow House, 2002
Garofalo Architects, Nothstine, study 2001

Page 35
Diller + Scofidio, Slow House, Long Island, 1991, model in the permanent collection of The Museum of Modern Art, New York City.

Page 36
Diller Scofidio, Slow House under construction, 1991, photograph courtesy of Diller + Scofidio.

Page 38
LOT/EK, MDU, 2001

Pages 40–41
LOT/EK, Morton Loft, New York, 1999, photograph by Paul Warchol

Page 42
Craig Konyk, Hydra(one), 2000

Page 44
Craig Konyk, The Distended Family Home, 2000

Page 46
Charles and Ray Eames, *Glimpses of the USA*, 1959, in the Moscow World's Fair Auditorium, Eames Archives, Library of Congress

Page 49
Charles and Ray Eames, *Glimpses of the USA*, 1959, Eames Archives, Library of Congress

Page 50
Michael Bell, Chrome House, 2000

Pages 52–53
Michael Bell, Duration House, 2000

Pages 54–57
Herzog & de Meuron, Kramlich Residence and Media Collection, Napa Valley, California, 2000-

Pages 58–59
Herzog & de Meuron, Leyman House, 2000, photograph by Margherita Spiluttini

Page 60
Neil Denari, Project for Vertical Smooth House, Los Angeles, 1997

Page 62
Neil Denari, Project for Corrugated Duct House, Palm Springs, California, 1998

Page 64
Mies van der Rohe, Tugendhat House, Brno, 1928–30

Page 67
Mies van der Rohe, ART166172: Riehl House. Potsdam-Neubabelsberg, Germany. c. 1907. View from lower garden. Photograph by William & Meyer Co., Chicago; The Mies van der Rohe Archive. (MI144). Digital Image © The Museum of Modern Art/Licensed by SCALA/Art Resource, NY.

Mies van der Rohe, ART166171: Riehl House. Potsdam-Neubabelsberg, Germany. ca. 1907. View of entrance facade. Photograph by William & Meyer Co., Chicago; The Mies van der Rohe Archive. (MI141)

Page 68
MVRDV, 100 WOZOCOS, Amsterdam-Osdorp, with Bureau Bouwkunde Rotterdam, The Netherlands, 1994–1997, photograph by Hans Werlemann, 1999

Page 70
MVRDV, plot 12 with Arno van der Mark, Two Houses in Borneo-Sporenbourg, 1996-2000, photographs by Nicholas Kane

Page 75
Chun-Huei Yang

Pages 76–77
David Mabbot

Page 78
Eric Samuels

Page 79
Yansong Ma, Tijana Vujosevic

Page 80
Eric Samuels

Page 81
Stella Papadopolous

Pages 82–83
Tim Phillips

Page 85
David Mabbott

Page 86
Chun-Huei Yang

Page 87
Yansong Ma

Pages 88–90
Tijana Vujosevic

Page 91
Adam Ruedig

Pages 92–94
Mark Foster Gage

Page 95
Tim Phillips

Pages 96–97
Stella Papadopoulos

Pages 100–101
Mark Foster Gage

Pages 102–3
David Mabbott

Pages 104–5
Can Tiryaki

Pages 106–7
Adam Ruedig

Pages 108–10
Chun-Huei Yang

Page 111
Alexander Hathaway

Page 112
Tijana Vujosevic

Pages 113–15
Eric Samuels

Pages 116–17
David Mabbott

Pages 118–19
Yansong Ma

Pages 120–21
Stella Papadopoulos

Pages 122–23
Adam Ruedig

Pages 124–25
Chun-Huei Yang

Pages 126–27
Yansong Ma

Pages 128–31
Michael Chung

Pages 132–33
Adam Ruedig

Pages 134–35
Chun-Huei Yang

Page 136
Michael Chung

Page 137
Mark Foster Gage

Pages 138–40
Alexander Hathaway

Page 141
Eric Samuels

Pages 142–43
Tim Phillips

Pages 144–47
Adam Ruedig

Page 148
Michael Chung

Page 149
Tim Phillips

Pages 150–51
Stella Papadopoulos

Pages 152–55
Mark Foster Gage

Pages 156–59
Tijana Vujosevic

Pages 160–63
David Mabbott

Pages 164–67
Chun-Huei Yang

Pages 168–71
Michael Chung

Pages 172–75
Stella Papadopoulos

Pages 176–79
Yansong Ma